D1036853

UTOPIA AND REALITY

UTOPIA AND REALITY

A COLLECTIVE PORTRAIT OF

AMERICAN SOCIALISTS

BETTY YORBURG

NEW YORK AND LONDON
COLUMBIA UNIVERSITY PRESS
1969

BETTY YORBURG is Assistant Professor in The Department of Sociology, The City College of The City University of New York.

FOR LEON

PREFACE

THIS collective portrait is a product of a series of tape-recorded interviews conducted over a period of eighteen months, in 1965 and 1966, with present and former leaders of the Socialist Party of America. The interview materials have been analyzed to reveal patterns in the attitudes, values and actions of three generations of high-echelon leaders of the Party. Differences among the generations have been related to certain changes that have taken place in American society since the turn of the century.

I want to thank Bernard Rosenberg, particularly, and Deborah Offenbacher, Arthur J. Vidich, and F. William Howton for their comments on earlier drafts of this book. John D. Moore, of Columbia University Press, has also been very helpful in offering suggestions for improving the manuscript.

Some time after beginning the interviews, I went to the Oral History Research Office at Columbia University to consult several reminiscences of Socialist Party leaders that are on file in the Oral History Collection. The Collection contains transcriptions of tape-recorded reminiscences of individuals who have been prominent in public life or in a particular field of work. Dr. Louis M. Starr, director of the Oral History Research Office, invited me to contribute my tapes to the Collection, where they would form a special collection on socialism in America.

I want to thank Mrs. Elizabeth B. Mason, also of the Oral History Office, and Dr. Starr for their interest in my work and their generosity in providing me with typescripts of my tapes. Without their help, the task of analysis would have been far more difficult—a systematic content analysis would have been almost impossible to do—and the richness and the accuracy of the direet quotations included in the book might have been diminished.

I regret that my father, who is no longer alive, will be unable to read this book. His intense interest in politics and our frequent political discussions during my childhood and adolescence inspired my interest in the subject of this study.

My husband, Dr. Leon Yorburg, has been a thoughtful listener through the years. I owe a great debt to him.

There remains a final expression of gratitude to the people whom I interviewed. They understood my purpose, and they believed in what I was doing. They were enthusiastic, and they were candid in their reminiscences beyond my most optimistic expectations. I shall think of them, from time to time, as kind and generous people whom I had the good fortune to encounter in my own search for answers to the riddles of time and of history.

BETTY YORBURG

Summer, 1968
Pelham, New York

CONTENTS

INTRODUCTION

SOCIALISM has been a focus of interest and investigation by a great number of scholars and writers, in this country and abroad, for over a hundred years. Literally thousands of books and articles have been written on socialism as a political movement or as an economic system, as well as on the doctrines, premises, and goals of various socialist movements, and the successes and failures of these movements. What contribution can another book on socialism make to the vast literature on this topic?

Social scientists, working in the tradition of Max Weber and Roberto Michels in sociology and Gustave Le Bon in social psychology, have developed a fairly impressive body of theory and knowledge about the origins, structure, and functioning of social movements, religious and secular, past and present. An aspect of these movements that tends to be relatively neglected, however, is the subjective meaning of social movements for those who are, or were, very actively involved and deeply committed to them—the shared attitudes, values, experiences, and world views of the members, as well as their publicly stated beliefs and their public actions.

The need for this type of knowledge has been noted by Daniel Bell:

To see history as changes in sensibilities and style or, more, how different classes of people mobilized their emotional energies and adopted different moral postures is novel; yet the history of moral temper is, I feel, one of the most important ways of understanding social change and, particularly, the irrational forces at work in men. . . . Most historians of social movements have been excessively "intellectualistic" -in that the emphasis has been on doctrine or on organizational technique, and less on emotional styles.[1]

Not only has the work of historians of the Socialist Party of America emphasized doctrines, issues, and external events, so have the published memoirs and biographies of leaders of the Party. The memoirs that are available do not contain much discussion in depth of how the authors came to join the Party, how Party membership changed their lives, their attitudes toward their comrades and their fellow men, toward the world in which they lived and the world in which they hoped to live. Since the younger leaders have not written memoirs, it is not possible to trace the thread of change in the quality of the life experiences of succeeding generations of leaders of the Socialist Party.

Thus, it is difficult to reconstruct the ethos of the Socialist Party over the years if one is limited to published memoirs and historical accounts of the Party.

Letter writing has become virtually a lost art with the use of the telephone for private communications, and memoirs are written for the public at large. The possibility of capturing the actual moral and emotional climate of social movements, therefore, is becoming increasingly difficult, particularly for scholars of the future.

It is largely this aspect of Socialist Party history, the emotional and moral dimensions of Party membership, that I shall attempt to portray and communicate through the use of direct quotations from a series of tape-recorded, loosely structured interviews conducted with former and present leaders of the Party. The leaders were asked to recall and discuss the influences and circumstances which led to their decision to join the Socialist Party, their initial

[1] Daniel Bell, *The End of Ideology.* Rev. Ed. (New York: The Free Press, 1962), p. 440.

conception of socialism and how this has changed (if it has), why the Party and the movement failed in this country, and their opinion of the future prospects for a socialist movement in America. This was the basic framework for the interviews. A great deal of additional material emerged because the interviews were essentially free-associational within the broad limits of the framework.

Since this will be a sociological analysis, a definition of the sociological perspective may be helpful. Difficult to define, it tends to vary with the particular sociologist. However, one feature that most sociological researches have in common is a focus on typical human behavior, particularly as this behavior is influenced by group life. Sociologists are concerned with recurring patterns in human behavior and the underlying attitudes, values, and beliefs that are shared by individuals in similar social locations. These social locations are largely determined by such factors as citizenship in a particular nation, economic class, race, religion, ethnic origin, occupation, education, rural-urban residence, age, and sex. Unlike the novelist, sociologists are bound by fact and scientific rules of evidence in their descriptions of social reality. These are the hallmarks of the sociological approach to understanding the world in which we live.

In the chapters that follow, the focus will be on similarities in the thinking, acting, and feelings of the respondents as they express their ideas and recall their life experiences. I have chosen to use the case study method in its most familiar form—life history materials—because I believe it is best suited to reveal changes through time and the relationship between ideas and behavior and the changing social context.

THE HYPOTHESIS OF THE STUDY

I began the interviews expecting that points of view and ideological conflicts would be patterned along generational lines, because people who are born and grow up during a particular time in history share certain common life experiences. The hypothesis derives from Karl Mannheim's concept of political generations:

> To mention only one of the many other possible bases of collective existence, out of which different interpretations of the world and different forms of knowledge may arise, we may point to the role played by the relationship between differently situated generations.
>
> This factor influences, in very many cases, the principles of selection, organization, and polarization of theories and points of view prevailing in a society at a given moment.[2]

The broad question underlying my inquiry was: Are there similarities in the viewpoints, perspectives, and life experiences of the leadership of the Party which vary along generational lines? More specifically, if the leaders are grouped into generational categories on the basis of the period of time during which they joined the Party, are there discernible patterns in their attitudes and beliefs regarding the failure and the future of socialism in this country? Are there generational patterns with regard to the stated influences which led them to join the movement? In their images of themselves? In their attitudes toward communism? In what they regard as the most urgent problems facing American society today? Have they been differentially affected by psychological theories of irrational motivation in political dissent?

Where patterns emerge along generational lines, I will relate these patterns to certain changes that have occurred in American society over the past seventy years, the period during which the leaders have been active in public life.

[2] Karl Mannheim, *Ideology and Utopia* (New York: Harcourt, Brace and Co., 1936), p. 270. Mannheim also discusses this concept in "The Problem of Generations," *Essays on the Sociology of Knowledge* (New York: Oxford University Press, 1952), pp. 276–322. In addition to Mannheim's work, other important papers which discuss attitudes and values along a generational axis include: Kingsley Davis, "The Sociology of Parent-Youth Conflict," *American Sociological Review*, 5 (August, 1940), 523–34; Talcott Parsons, "Age and Sex in the Social Structure of the United States," *American Sociological Review*, 7 (October, 1942), 604–16; and Bruno Bettelheim, "The Problem of Generations," in Erik H. Erikson, ed., *Youth: Change and Challenge* (New York: Basic Books, 1963), pp. 64–92.

THE SOCIALIST PARTY—PAST AND PRESENT

For those who are not familiar with Socialist Party history, a very brief sketch will serve to provide a background for reading the quoted interview materials and will give some indication of the place of the Socialist Party in the history of American politics.[3]

The Socialist Party of America was founded at Indianapolis, Indiana, in 1901. It originally consisted of an amorphous, and—compared to contemporary left-wing organizations—incredibly diversified coalition of regional groups: garment workers from New York, sharecroppers from Oklahoma, railroad workers from Indiana, brewery workers from Milwaukee, and miners and lumberjacks from the Pacific Northwest. The early Party organization contained Christian socialists and millionaires, intellectuals and immigrant workers, farmers, pacifists, and a handful of Negroes.

Except for those from the East, most of the delegates to the first convention were not Marxists. Their radical orientations stemmed from previous membership in the Populist Party, the Bellamy Clubs, Eugene Victor Debs' American Railway Union, and other dissident organizations in American society.

The Eastern members, in particular those from New York, were largely ex-members of the Socialist Labor Party, then under the leadership of Daniel De Leon. These socialists had become dissatisfied with De Leon's rigid and doctrinaire position with regard to Marxist theory and practice. The Easterners emphasized parliamentary political action, social reforms or "immediate demands" to be achieved within the capitalist system, and a gradual evolution of the United States into a socialist economic system. The socialist state was envisioned as one in which industries would be collectively owned, the economic needs of all citizens would be provided for, and income distribution would be equalitarian.

[3] This account is based on a number of sources. An unusually good history of the Socialist Party is: David A. Shannon, *The Socialist Party of America* (New York: Macmillan Co., 1955).

The Westerners, particularly those from the Rocky Mountains and the Pacific Northwest, shared the same vision of a socialist state, but were more radical and impatient in their approach to socialism. Bill Haywood and the Industrial Workers of the World advocated a form of syndicalism verging on anarchy. There were varying statements of this position. Essentially, it involved the organization of all workers into one great nationwide union, a revolutionary general strike, the assumption of political power by the union, and the establishment of a socialist economy.

The Party grew very rapidly from 1901 to 1912. In the election of 1912, its presidential candidate, Eugene Victor Debs, polled 900,672 votes, 6 per cent of the popular vote.[4] Through the first eleven years of its existence, the Party succeeded in electing a number of reform-oriented local administrations in small towns and cities across the nation from Flint, Michigan, to Milwaukee, Wisconsin, to Berkeley, California.

The first reversal in Party fortunes occurred in 1913 with the departure of Bill Haywood and many of his Western followers. The advocacy of sabotage and "direct action" by this group had always been distasteful to the less militant Easterners. The issue finally resulted in this first splitting off of a major faction within the Party.

The election of Woodrow Wilson further weakened the Party. A number of intellectuals in the Party joined the Wilson administration to help participate in the new reforms that were being enacted.

World War I was an additional factor of some magnitude in the progressive erosion of Party strength. The Party's position condemning the war resulted in the departure of more members, particularly among the intellectuals. Wartime repressions also weakened the Party considerably. Socialist Party newspapers were censored and banned. Its leaders were fined and imprisoned for obstructing the draft. The banning of Party newspapers was

[4] United States Bureau of the Census, *Historical Statistics of the United States, Colonial Times to 1957* (Washington, D.C.: Government Printing Office, 1960), p. 682.

particularly damaging to Western rural Party organizations since they were cut off from communication with National Headquarters. The Oklahoma Party organization, for example, which had polled a greater percentage of the state votes (16 per cent) in 1912 than had the Party in any other state in the nation, had only seventy-two paid up members in 1922.[5] The even more severe repressions of the postwar "red scare" period in America, a reaction to the Russian Revolution, also took their toll.

In 1912, the Socialist Party had 117,984 paid members.[6] By 1922, membership had declined to 11,277.[7] Membership continued to decline slightly with each succeeding year in the 1920s, until the depression. The relative prosperity of the twenties hindered the recruitment of new members. Also, potential young recruits preferred joining the more militant communist organizations in existence by that time.

The Communist Labor Party and the Communist Party were formed after the Russian Revolution by dissident left-wing elements in the Socialist Party who believed that revolution in America was imminent. They rejected the Socialist Party emphasis on parliamentary action, gradual social reforms, and eventual evolution into socialism.

Conditions in post-World War I America, however, did not portend a forthcoming revolution. Trade unions were not revolutionary; they were striving for legitimation and respectability within the capitalist system. The country had become a creditor nation and was experiencing an era of prosperity.

The Socialist Party survived the declining years of the 1920s supported largely by committed and resolute members in the East. Eugene Debs died in 1926. He was succeeded by Norman Matoon Thomas, an ordained Presbyterian minister who had left the church to seek a political application of Christian ethics.

Since 1912 the Socialist Party had taken on an increasingly conservative aspect. With the departure of many of the Western-

[5] Shannon, *The Socialist Party of America*, p. 111.
[6] *Ibid.*, p. 163.
[7] *Ibid.*, p. 163.

ers in 1913 and the withdrawal of more militant elements who left to form various communist organizations, Party membership became more homogeneous. This was reflected not only in avowed policies but also in the regional and social origins of the membership. The Party leadership through the years also reflected this increasing homogenization.

Eugene Debs had come from the labor movement, had little formal education, and appealed largely to the working class. Norman Thomas, the son of a Presbyterian minister, was an intellectual and appealed most effectively to intellectuals.

The 1928 National Executive Committee of the Party, elected when Thomas was nominated for the presidency of the United States for the first time, contained only one person who had been a laborer in his early years, no one from a rural area, and no one who, at any time, had been associated with more radical elements in the Party.[8] The Party had taken giant steps toward the monolithic sectarianism which characterized its later years.

The depression gave new impetus to Socialist Party activities. Membership revived and Socialist Party candidates were elected in a number of municipal elections. The Socialist Party platforms of 1928 and 1932 advocated policies such as unemployment compensation, old-age pensions, child-labor laws and public works programs—policies which were later enacted into law by the Roosevelt administration.

New factional alignments appeared within the Party during the early years of the depression. The two major factions were known as the Old Guard and the Militants. The Old Guard were middle- and old-aged veterans of the Party who controlled most of the formal positions of leadership. They came, mainly, from New York, Pennsylvania, and Connecticut. The Militants were radical, doctrinaire Marxists who had entered the Party after the depression. Many of them were under thirty, and they rejected gradual reforms and parliamentary action as strategies for achieving a socialist state.

In the 1932 elections, the Socialist Party achieved its greatest

[8] *Ibid.*, p. 192.

electoral success under the leadership of Norman Thomas. However, his popular vote did not equal that of Eugene Debs in 1912. After 1932, the enactment of the New Deal reforms and the formal splitting off of the Old Guard weakened the Party considerably.

The New Deal program siphoned off many of the Party's talented intellectuals who wanted to participate in the enactment and implementation of welfare state measures.

The Old Guard left the Party in 1936 because they were unwilling to cooperate with the Communist Party in a united front. They formed the Social Democratic Federation in New York, Pennsylvania, Connecticut, and Maryland. Subsequently, they supported the Democratic Party at the national level.

The loss to the Party in this latest split was particularly grave, since much of its financial support had come from its veteran members, particularly in New York. The withdrawal of the garment industry unions, along with the Old Guard, left the Party almost without labor support.

The Party's unpopular stand on World War II resulted in an additional loss of membership. Before Pearl Harbor, the top Party leadership advocated neutrality, arguing that aid to the allies would lead to involvement in the war. After the United States entered the war, the Party took a position of "critical support" of the war. The American Socialist Party, like many of its Social Democratic counterparts in Europe, was not able to come to terms with the problem of meeting force with force in resistance to totalitarian opposition.

The Socialist Party ceased nationwide electoral activity in 1952 after a humiliatingly poor showing at the polls. Membership figures have remained relatively stable in recent years. In 1968 the Party is said to have approximately 7,500 members and to have experienced a slight increase in membership (13 per cent) during the past three years.[9]

The role of the Party, as it is presently defined by its members,

[9] These figures were obtained from the National Headquarters of the Socialist Party.

is that of an educational organization actively engaged in an effort to bring to public attention information about problems which American society faces.

Norman Thomas, in one of his last formulations of the Party's role in American politics described the Party's present functions metaphorically. It is to act as a yeast in the fermentation of radical social change—change which is to be brought about, if at all, by attempts to influence the activities of the established political parties in this country.[10]

Obviously the Socialist Party and the socialist movement have had far more publicity and notoriety in this country than a brief accounting of official membership figures and popular votes suggests is justified. Throughout its history there have been many self-defined, unaffiliated socialists that Party membership rosters do not indicate. A number of these socialists unaffiliated with the Party were writers and other individuals who were close to the sources of mass communication. This may account for public misconceptions regarding the actual strength of socialist organizations in this country in the past. The Communist Party, for example, never received more than 100,000 votes in national elections, even at its height in the 1930s.[11]

The Socialist Party arose in response to certain felt needs, primarily economic but also ethical, as we shall see. It floundered for a variety of reasons which will be discussed in Chapter III. Its effects on American political and economic life can never be determined with precision. The only statement that can be made with confidence is that American society has changed dramatically since the time of the founding of the Socialist Party, and contemporary social movements have also changed in significant ways.

---

10 Norman Thomas, *Socialism Re-examined* (New York: W. W. Norton and Co., 1963).

11 In 1932, William Z. Foster received 102,785 presidential votes. No other candidate, running under the Communist Party banner, ever again achieved this vote. See United States Bureau of the Census, *Historical Statistics*, p. 682.

THE CHANGING SOCIAL CONTEXT
OF POLITICAL DISSENT

It is not my intention to write a history of intellectual thought or to discuss in detail the major predicaments of our age and the major existential issues that confront us. Over the past seventy years, however, there have been certain changes in intellectual orientations and social conditions in America that have affected the values and goals of political dissenters in our society. These changes bear on the findings of this book and should be kept in mind.

At its inception in 1901, the Socialist Party of America operated in an atmosphere of ebullient optimism. Issues were clear-cut and polarized. Good and evil seemed unambiguous. Belief in the possibility of unlimited rationalism and the elimination of conflict in human relationships was unequivocal. The identity of the mass base which was to provide political support for effecting radical social change was not questioned; it was the wage worker. The ultimate goals of socialism and the characteristics of a socialist economic system were also undisputed: collective ownership of productive property and distribution according to the principle of human need. Socialism, for these early socialists, was simply an extension into the economic sphere of the rationalism of the humanists of the Renaissance and the Enlightenment. The belief in the inevitability of socialism, which was widespread among the leadership and the rank and file at that time, rested on belief in unlimited social progress and the perfectibility of man.

Since the turn of the century, increasing industrialization and urbanization in this country have been accompanied by a continuously expanding rate of social change, a constant growth in the complexity of the social structure, and the bureaucratization of all spheres of life, with the exception of the family.

The pace of social change is constantly accelerating because modern technology provides an abundance of new elements to be combined in new ways, cultural borrowing and diffusion are facilitated by improved transportation and communication and social movements, emphasizing new norms and values, proliferate.

Bureaucracy expands because the scope of tasks to be performed in complex societies is constantly growing, and administrators, coordinators, and managers also proliferate.

The bureaucratization of our society has resulted in what Robert MacIver has characterized as a "great new world of means without ends." [12] There is an increasing concentration of power, decision-making, and expertise at the top of the various institutional hierarchies, and an increasing concentration on means at the middle and lower levels.

This is reflected in the fact that long-range and far-reaching goals tend to be repudiated by groups currently engaged in efforts to effect radical social change. The New Left, for example, as distinct from the Old Left, is characterized by a militant pragmatism. The emphasis has been on community organization around immediate objectives for improving the lives of the poor: better housing, jobs and education, the elimination of police brutality, and issues of pressing concern to students such as peace in Vietnam and university reform.[13]

Milton Gordon has noted a similar lack of long-range goals in organizations dedicated to improving the status of minority groups in this country.[14] The emphasis in these organizations is not on long-range questions of social structure and social change, but on combating specific and concrete instances of racial and religious discrimination.

A similar shift has also taken place in the peace movement in this country, away from the long-range goal of permanent peace to "discrete bite-sized, yet coordinated individual actions along a broad front of community affairs." [15]

---

[12] Robert MacIver, "The Great Emptiness," in Eric and Mary Josephson, eds., *Man Alone* (New York: Dell Publishing Co., 1962), p. 145.

[13] Paul Jacobs and Saul Landau, eds., *The New Radicals* (New York: Vintage Books, 1966).

[14] Milton M. Gordon, *Assimilation in American Life* (New York: Oxford University Press, 1964).

[15] Theodore Olson, "The New Peace Effort: Sociology Overcoming Ide-

In addition to a general trend toward ritualism in a highly bureaucratized society, a factor often cited to explain the current apotheosis of means in our society is the advent of the atomic era. It is difficult to commit oneself to long-range goals when the long-range fate of mankind is in question.

Current attempts to effect radical social change are also plagued by the blurring of issues and meanings which occurs with increasing complexity of social structure and technology. The capitalist of old, the captain of industry and proprietor of the family firm, who broke up strikes with Pinkerton men and the militia, is now bifurcated into manager and stockholder. Is the manager a technocrat, hired on the basis of merit, and dedicated to the good of company and country? Or, is he profiteer, price fixer and manipulator of colleagues, government, and public for the purpose of furthering his own self-interest? Is he flesh and blood villain or nameless pasteboard image constructed by skilled public relations retainers?

Good and evil are no longer the concrete and unalloyed phenomena that they were in the days of early capitalism and early socialism.

In contrast to the past, not only are objects of attack blurred and hidden in contemporary society, but meanings of slogans and goals are also blurred. Even in a society in which the citizenry have traditionally been prone to organizing in response to felt needs, the past six or seven years in America have been characterized by an extraordinary amount of sloganizing and unrest. Fictions and realities are colliding publicly, and reexaminations are flourishing. New political formulas and visions of utopia have appeared in an abundance appropriate to the age: The New Frontier, The War on Poverty, The Great Society, Participatory Democracy, Counter Community, Black Power, White Power, Blue Power, and Student Power, to mention but a few in the constantly changing vocabulary of all strata in the society.

What has decreased proportionately is clarity of meaning in the

---

ology," Arthur B. Shostak, ed., *Sociology in Action* (Homewood, Illinois: Dorsey Press, 1966), p. 306.

new ideologies, or fragments of ideology. What does socialism mean today? Or, Freedom Now? Or, Black Power? One now has to ask additional questions such as, Freedom for what? Or, Black Power for what? The slogans of early socialism such as Bread, Land, and Peace seem anachronistically simple by comparison.

The potential mass base for support of radical social change is also problematic in contemporary industrial societies. Traditional socialist parties, including the American Socialist Party, sought support from the industrial worker. Conservative parties sought support from the upper class and, also, from the old middle class which consisted of self-employed businessmen, farmers, and independent professionals. The old middle class valued its independence and its property and favored *laissez-faire* economic policies.

As C. Wright Mills has pointed out, however, the bureaucratization of economic life has changed the circumstances of the old middle class.[16] They have lost their independence. They now work as dependent salaried employees in large organizations—as managers, professionals, salespeople, and office workers. Furthermore, contrary to Karl Marx's prediction, they are growing in numbers relative to the working class.

As dependent salaried employees, the new middle class shares certain interests with the working class, interests in social security and other welfare state measures and in government economic planning to avoid depression and inflation. Because of this similarity of interests, in recent years parties on the left have adopted measures calculated to obtain the support of this class. Parties on the right, wishing also to obtain their support, have tended to support welfare state measures, up to a point. The resulting narrowing of appeals by parties on the right and the left, predicated

16 C. Wright Mills, *White Collar* (New York: Oxford University Press, 1951), Chapter V, documents this shift in the middle class from self-employed to salaried status and from production to service types of occupations; Reinhard Bendix, *Work and Authority in Industry* (New York: Harper & Row, 1963), Chapter IV, cites additional evidence of the increasing shift from entrepreneurial to administrative functions in the United States, France, Great Britain, Germany, and Sweden in the past century.

on a changing mass base, is the basis for the presumed consensus in party politics in America which social scientists have labeled a decline or an "end of ideology." [17]

The fact of an end or a decline in ideology is accepted by many social scientists even at the present time of heightened sloganizing and rhetoric. It has been argued, for example, that the increased application of "scientific criteria" in policy-making attenuates the effects of ideology.[18] It could, however, be argued that scientific criteria may be used in policy-making to implement ideologically determined policies.

Ideology, either broadly defined as a set of doctrines which formulates group perspectives, or more narrowly defined as a set of ideas that justifies and preserves a particular social system,[19] has not declined, and has certainly not disappeared. It would be more accurate, given modern conditions of extremely rapid social change and the bureaucratization of almost all spheres of life, to refer to a corresponding change in the quality of group ideologies. Goals and their rationalizing doctrines are increasingly concrete and short-range (reflecting the complexity of social life and the concentration of power at the top of the various institutional hierarchies) and are constantly shifting (reflecting the exigencies of rapid social change and of rapidly changing publics in an era of instant communication)

To return to the question of the right or left inclinations of the middle class, historically, the old middle class has supported conservative parties and, in times of crisis, fascist parties. Mussolini attributed the initial success of his Italian fascist movement to the

[17] See, Edward Shils, "The End of Ideology?", *Encounter*, 5 (November, 1955), 52–58; Daniel Bell, *The End of Ideology* (New York: The Free Press, 1962), pp. 393–407; and Seymour Martin Lipset, *Political Man* (Garden City, New York: Doubleday and Co., 1960), Chapter XIII.

[18] Robert E. Lane, "The Decline of Politics and Ideology in a Knowledgeable Society," *American Sociological Review*, 31 (October, 1966), 649–62.

[19] For this conception of the term ideology, see Karl Mannheim, *Ideology and Utopia* (New York: Harcourt, Brace and Co., 1936), pp. 55–60. Mannheim used the term utopia in a non-invidious sense, as it is used in the title of this book, to refer to complexes of ideas which direct activity toward changing the prevailing social order. *Ibid.*, p. 192.

support of small property owners in the Po area.[20] The appeal of the German fascist movement to the old middle class has been documented in numerous sources.[21]

Whether the new middle class will opt for radical parties or policies in the future is problematical. In discussing the question, it is necessary to separate the economic values of the new middle class from other values they are known to possess.

While the new middle class may favor economic reforms, there is some question about their future position on the question of civil rights and civil liberties, particularly in the lower-middle class. Samuel Stouffer, in a nationwide sample of five thousand Americans, found that verbalizations of intolerance and social status (as measured by occupation), were inversely related.[22] Richard Hofstadter and others have pointed out that many members of the lower-middle class (and the working class), and many socially mobile individuals are most apt to experience status insecurity and, therefore, are most likely to feel threatened by the upward push of new minorities.[23] They may thus tend to favor the stress on respectability and the restriction of civil liberties that conservative parties emphasize at the expense of economic reforms. Conservative parties in democratic countries tend to deflect attention from economic issues by stressing patriotism and traditional morality and exploiting noneconomic bases of social cleavage such as religious, ethnic, and racial differences. A recent illustration of this phenomenon is the stand on the question of the "colored peoples" by some members of the Conservative Party in England.

[20] Erwin von Beckerath, "Fascism," in *Encyclopedia of the Social Sciences*, Vol. VI (New York: Macmillan Co., 1937).

[21] See for example: Hans Gerth, "The Nazi Party: Its Leadership and Composition," in Robert K. Merton, ed., *Reader in Bureaucracy* (Glencoe, Illinois: The Free Press, 1952); also Rudolph Heberle, *From Democracy to Nazism* (Baton Rouge, Louisiana: Louisiana State University Press, 1945), which describes the attraction of small farm proprietors in Schleswig-Holstein to the Nazi Party.

[22] Samuel Stouffer, *Communism, Conformity and Civil Liberties* (New York: Doubleday and Co., 1955).

[23] Richard Hofstadter, "The Pseudo-Conservative Revolt (1955)" in Daniel Bell, ed., *The Radical Right* (New York: Doubleday and Co., 1962), pp. 63–80.

At the present time there is no unanimity of opinion on the subject of which class, or classes, shall form the base of support for radical social change. Not only do leaders of political organizations seeking this type of change differ, but social scientists and other intellectuals also differ on this question. C. Wright Mills, writing in the early 1950s, predicted that the white collar worker, increasingly proletarianized by the automation of his work activities and increasingly unionized, would affiliate with the wage worker to support radical economic reforms.[24] By 1961, however, in one of his last published statements, Mills impatiently repudiated his earlier judgment and called upon the "young intelligentsia" to act as "an immediate agency of radical social change."[25] Mill's young intelligentsia, now known as the New Left, has meanwhile turned to a new mass base which is neither industrial worker, nor farmer, nor middle class. It is for the first time the lowest income group in our society, the poor—Negro, Puerto Rican, and White.

This stratum, variously labeled the lower class, the lower-lower class, the poor, the unstable working class, the culturally deprived and disadvantaged, and the hard-to-reach—the profusion of terms perhaps reflecting the discomfort of those who deal with them—consists of people who are unskilled and permanently unemployed, underemployed, or irregularly employed. They have a high incidence of desertion, divorce, illegitimacy, alcoholism, drug addiction, juvenile delinquency, and mental illness.

In an automating society, there is a tendency for this lowest, unskilled stratum to harden and perpetuate itself in stable, if not increasing, misery. Education is essential for social mobility in such a society. Talcott Parsons,[26] Suzanne Keller,[27] and other sociologists have emphasized that structural pressures of the economy toward increasing efficiency and rationalism have

[24] Mills, *White Collar*, pp. 319–20.
[25] C. Wright Mills, "Letter to the New Left," *Studies on the Left*, Vol. 2, No. 1, 1961, p. 66.
[26] Talcott Parsons, *Structure and Process in Modern Societies* (Glencoe, Illinois: The Free Press, 1960).
[27] Suzanne Keller, *Beyond the Ruling Class* (New York: Random House, 1963).

tended to foster equality of opportunity in highly industrialized societies. They claim that ascriptive criteria such as family and race are replaced by achievement criteria such as merit and talent in the recruitment process.

This is true largely for the middle class and, to a lesser extent, for the working class. The overwhelming weight of the evidence collected in recent years, however, indicates that the children of the poor do not typically encounter the intellectual, emotional, or moral climate that fosters academic achievement. Teachers, for example, tend to view urban slum children as inferior and incapable of learning.[28] This can become a self-fulfilling prophecy for these children.

Educational aspirations of children tend to be very highly associated with the amount of parental education. In a nationwide survey of 35,000 high school seniors, it was found that students with high ability from families with the lowest educational and occupational status were half as likely to plan to attend college as students of similar ability from homes where the parents had achieved a high level of education.[29] The cycle of dependence is now a banality in the vocabulary of reporters and public officials in our society.

The traditional political apathy of the lowest stratum of our society, or at least a part of this stratum, has been modified recently as a result of the broadening of the horizons that occurs with urbanization and exposure to the mass media. Whether this stratum will form the mass base for truly radical measures of economic reform, however, is uncertain. Reforms from above tend to co-opt the appeals of political organizations of the left to a greater extent than in the past. On the other hand, the confluence of race and poverty in our society may obviate governmental efforts to maintain order by gradual and limited reforms.

[28] Mel Ravitz, "The Role of the School in the Urban Setting," in A. Harry Passow, ed., *Education in Depressed Areas* (New York: Teachers College Bureau of Publications, 1963).

[29] Natalie Rogoff, "Local Social Structure and Educational Selection," in A. H. Halsey, et al., eds., *Education, Economy and Society* (New York: The Free Press, 1961).

Urban race riots seem to be related more to changing subjective states of optimism about the future, than to the quality and quantity of efforts to provide relief that are made by government and private agencies.[30] This brings us to the fact of the decline, if not the end, of the American Dream, the belief that success is available to everyone in American society, and that failure is a matter of individual responsibility. Insofar as the American Dream has had an inhibiting effect on radical political action in the past, its decline may herald a greater radicalization of lower income groups in the population.

The question, however, of which strata will support what kind of change and when, if at all, is highly speculative and subject to much informal disputation among leaders of contemporary political organizations or groups seeking radical change in our society.

The initial certainty of the Socialist Party about the inevitability of socialism and the agents of socialist change is gone. This can be illustrated by a quotation from the writings of Norman Thomas, leader of the Socialist Party for over forty years:

As I read over what I have been writing and think of the experiences through which I have lived, I am aware that in my re-examination of socialism, I have laid no emotional basis for a great mass movement, such as those which have sometimes changed the face of history. I have offered challenge rather than certitude. I have been skeptical of infallible dogmas. I have assured no class, race, or nation of its messianic destiny.[31]

Beliefs about the potentialities for rationalism in the conduct of human affairs and the possibility of eliminating conflict and aggression in social life have also changed markedly since the turn of the century. These changed attitudes stem largely from a series of disillusioning external events that have taken place in the past fifty years.

World War I was particularly disillusioning to the international

[30] Kurt Lang and Gladys E. Lang, "Racial Disturbances as Collective Protests," unpublished paper read at the 62nd annual meeting of the American Sociological Association, August, 1967.
[31] Norman Thomas, *Socialism Re-examined* p. 306.

socialist movement, which witnessed workers of separate nations fighting for their kings and presidents against workers of other nations. With the depression came mass unemployment and starvation, existing side by side with the widespread destruction of unsaleable livestock and crops. Totalitarian states arose—of the left, as well as the right. The Stalinist purges of the 1930s, the Hitler-Stalin Pact, the Hungarian uprising in 1956, and Nikita Khrushchev's revelations after Stalin's death, about the injustices of the Stalin regime, added their toll to the progressive disenchantment of political radicals in this country. The legacy of the Enlightenment and the assumptions about the beneficent potentialities of mass education were shattered when Germany, a nation with a very high level of education, engaged in mass killing on a scale unparalleled in history. Knowledge and modern technology enhanced and refined the techniques of violence and brutality. World War II has been followed by a series of lesser wars. At the present time, visions of a classless, frictionless, and conflict-free society seem unrealistic in the light of accumulating historical experience and increased knowledge about the human personality.

The popularization of the theories of Sigmund Freud and his followers, who had emphasized the role of intrapsychic conflict in human behavior, has tended to diminish confidence, at least among some intellectuals, in the assumption that economic adjustments can completely resolve the problem of human aggression. In Freud's words, "Agressiveness was not created by property." [32] Freud focused on individual conflicts and their intrafamilial origins. He did not believe that changes in the social structure could appreciably alter the character of individuals in a society.

Freud's emphasis on unconscious motivation and the ubiquitous presence of irrational forces in man's relationship to man had

[32] Sigmund Freud, "Civilization and Its Discontents," *The Standard Edition of the Complete Psychological Works of Sigmund Freud* (London: The Hogarth Press, 1961), Vol. XXI, p. 113. Translated and edited by James Strachey.

a massive impact on intellectuals and artists in this country. We can only speculate as to the reasons for the success of Freudian theory in America. The psychoanalytic treatment process is based on the principles of self-improvement and is congenial with American traditions of individualism. The emphasis in psychoanalytic theory is on unconscious conflicts and the crippling effects of these conflicts on individual functioning. A society which has emphasized individual responsibility in success may have found a theory which removes the onus of individual responsibility for failure particularly attractive. The individual is regarded as a victim of unconscious forces and a product of early formative experiences over which he had little control. In any case, the widespread acceptance of the theory in this country was a further disillusioning factor of great consequence. Altruism became unbelievable, and idealism became unfashionable.

The influence of Freudian theory in the 1930s led to what Talcott Parsons has called a psychological era in the United States.[33] Human motivation became a very popular focus of concern on the part of American intellectuals. The motivation of political radicals, particularly the attribution of irrational motivating factors to their political behavior, became an intellectual vogue—a vogue which has only recently diminished in popularity. The effects of the psychological era on the thinking and self-images of some of our respondents will be described in Chapter II.

Regardless of whether aggression is viewed as an instinctual drive or as a reactive response to frustration, conflict and aggression in a society are now generally recognized as stemming from multiple sources and not solely from differences in economic interests. For example, Ralf Dahrendorf[34] makes the point that whatever the extent of economic equality in a society, authority will always be unequally distributed throughout the social struc-

[33] Talcott Parsons, "Some Problems Confronting Sociology as a Profession," *American Sociological Review*, 24 (August, 1959), 547–59.

[34] Ralf Dahrendorf, *Class and Class Conflict in Industrial Society* (Stanford, California: Stanford University Press, 1959).

ture. Inequalities in authority generate antagonism and hostility, and social conflict, therefore, is intrinsic to social life.

Not only Freudian psychologists, but social scientists generally are now routinely taking note of unpredictable and irrational factors in their analyses of contemporary social life.

There is far greater awareness now of the complexity of the problem of predicting social change and of the great number of variables that must be taken into account: traditional attitudes and values, prejudices, biases, superstitions, levels of aspirations and religious, racial, and ethnic identifications as well as class commitments, to mention but a few. The problem of comprehending the laws of history is far more complex than Karl Marx and the early socialists envisioned. And the problem of eliminating conflict and human aggression in social life is far more implacable than they imagined.

THE LEADERS:
DEMOGRAPHIC CHARACTERISTICS [35]

AGE: The thirty-four leaders interviewed range in age from thirty-two to ninety. Their division into three broad categories is based on the time they joined the Party. The oldest leaders, *The World War I Generation,* joined the Party before, during, or within a few years of the end of World War I. This category has seventeen respondents. The second group, the *Interwar Generation,* joined the Party in the late 1920s or early 1930s. The nine leaders in this category spent their most active and influential years in the Party during the depression. *The World War II Generation* joined the Party shortly before, during, or after World War II. This group of eight respondents includes two leaders who joined the Party during the McCarthy era in the early 1950s.

The World War I Generation ranges in age from sixty to ninety; the Interwar Generation from forty-seven to fifty-five; and

[35] Appendix A contains a discussion of the problem of the representativeness of the sample.

the World War II Generation from thirty-two to forty-two. There is no overlap in age between the categories and, therefore, the classification can be said to represent distinct generations.

With respect to age at joining and age at which full-time Party activities were undertaken, in each succeeding generation the average age at which full-time Party activity was undertaken increases. This probably has to do, in part, with the increasingly middle-class nature of the leadership in the succeeding generations. A number of the oldest leaders were manual laborers in their youth. None of the leaders in the two younger generations has been a laborer except as a temporary expedient.

The period of adolescence terminated sooner for many of the World War I Generation. They began their full-time political activities at an earlier age. Most of the Interwar Generation joined the Party as part-time workers while in high school; a few joined in college. All of the youngest generation joined the Party while in college. Those who have worked full-time for the Party began this work after completing their college education.

EDUCATION: The World War I Generation is the most heterogeneous in educational background. This generation contains lawyers, ministers, and Ph.D.'s, as well as leaders who did not complete grade school. The two younger generations show a pattern of increasing homogeneity. There are few professionals, but almost all have had some college education. The youngest generation are all college graduates.

These trends in the educational characteristics of the leadership also reflect the increasingly middle-class homogeneous nature of the Party. In addition, they probably reflect changing conditions in our society. The increasing minimum level of education reflects the greater prevalence of a high school education in our society today. The decline in leaders with higher professional degrees in the two younger generations is probably a result of the depression, and also the rising standards in professional education in our society. Most of the oldest leaders obtained their professional degrees in night school, while engaged in full-time employment. It has become far more difficult to obtain professional degrees in night school over the years. The demands of political activism and the demands of professional training are not as easily reconciled as they once were.

ETHNIC ORIGINS: The majority of the leaders are of Eastern or Central European ancestry and Jewish religious origins; the rest are of Northern European or English descent and Protestant origins. There are fewer leaders of Protestant background, relatively, in the younger generations.

The attraction of individuals of Jewish descent to radical or liberal organizations can be explained on several grounds. Robert Park [36] pointed to their marginality in the societies in which they have lived. This condition enhances detachment and may promote the tendency to examine critically, and possibly reject, the dominant norms and values of these societies. As a relatively advantaged minority group, Jews also often experience what has been called status inconsistency.[37] In the ranking of the various criteria that determine overall social status, they stand high in education, income, and occupation, but low on religion and ethnic origin. Individuals who experience status inconsistency tend to desire extensive changes in the distribution of power in a society.[38] The need of some Jews for a functional equivalent of religion is another possible reason for their attraction to radical social movements, particularly to socialism.

Aside from these more general reasons, the preponderance of Jewish leaders in the sample has to do with the history of the Socialist Party in America. As I pointed out earlier, the original composition of the Party represented a regional coalition of East

[36] Robert E. Park, *Race and Culture* (Glencoe, Illinois: The Free Press, 1950).

[37] Gerhard Lenski, "Status Crystallization: A Non-Vertical Dimension of Social Status," *American Sociological Review*, 19 (August, 1954), 405–13.

[38] Erving Goffman, "Status Consistency and Preference for Change in Power Distribution," *American Sociological Review*, 22 (June, 1957), 275–81.

and West. The strongest Eastern base was in New York. The rank and file consisted largely of Jewish immigrant workers in the garment industry. The Jewish leaders in our sample are all either Eastern or Central European immigrants or descendents of immigrants, who were born in New York. The tradition of socialism and socialist activity was transplanted from Europe, and the older Jewish leaders in our study were very often socialized into the movement by family and neighborhood peer groups, as we shall see in Chapter II.

The slight tendency for the leadership to be more consistently Jewish in the younger generations probably has to do with the fact that the main organizational strength of the Party as it began to decline after the first World War, shifted gradually to New York.

While some of the older leaders were born in Europe, all of the leaders in the two younger generations were born in the United States. This is probably related to the extreme decline in immigration from Eastern Europe with the passage of the Immigration Act of 1924.

MARITAL STATUS: Almost all of the oldest leaders are married; there are no divorces in this generation. In each of the two younger generations, several leaders are divorced or separated. This undoubtedly reflects marital trends in the population at large—the increased instability of marriages resulting from the shift from institution to companionship, familism to individualism, and duty to happiness as the central outlook or expectation of participants in contemporary marriages.

MAJOR OCCUPATION: Some of the leaders are retired, of course. others have shown occupational mobility during the course of their lifetime. The following information has to do with the occupations in which the leaders have spent the major portion of their lives. These occupations fall into four categories: officials in nonprofit, interest or service organizations (political party, union, civil rights, pacifist, welfare), professionals (lawyers, teachers, academicians), writers (free lance, journalists, editors) and business. The two older generations are concentrated in employment in nonprofit interest or service organizations. The youngest generation has tended to shift to occupations in the fields of education and writing. This parallels the change in the functioning of the Socialist Party over the years from a political organization actively engaged in a struggle to obtain political power, to an educational organization interested primarily in bringing to public attention possible solutions to contemporary social problems.

SOCIALIST PARTY MEMBERSHIP: Generational differences also appear with regard to the present status of the leaders in relation to the Socialist Party. The Interwar Generation has been much more apt to drop out of the Party than have the other two generations. This is especially interesting in that it is this generation, the depression generation, that has been characterized by Lewis Feuer [39] and others as particularly disillusioned and estranged. We shall see whether these leaders show a pattern of greater disenchantment and pessimism than the other generations with respect to their present conception of socialism and their expectations for the future of socialism in this country.

Whether or not they are still members of the Party, and a little over half of the leaders still do belong to the Party, not one person answered, "No, not at all," when asked, "Would you still consider yourself a socialist?" Two answered no to the question, but one professes a residual distaste for capitalism, and the other retains vague pro-socialist feelings. The remaining leaders still consider themselves socialists, even those who have been out of the Party for many years.

In this brief summation of trends in the demographic characteristics of the leaders we see reflected the shift in the Socialist Party, over the years, to an increasingly middle-class, urban,

[39] Lewis Feuer, "What is Alienation? The Career of a Concept," in Maurice Stein and Arthur Vidich, eds., *Sociology on Trial* (Englewood Cliffs, New Jersey: Prentice-Hall, 1963), pp. 127–48.

Eastern, and native-born leadership. We also see that the self-definition as a socialist has persisted for the vast majority of the respondents and transcends present political affiliations. This fact will be quite apparent in the quotations from the interviews in suceeding chapters.

The pages that follow are divided into an initial chapter on the self-images of the leaders and three additional chapters corresponding to the major questions that were asked in the interviews. The Conclusion will contain a short summary of the findings and a discussion of possible implications of these findings for an understanding of contemporary political protest movements. The Appendixes contain a description of the interview, sampling, and content analysis procedures and a list of the coding variables used in the content analysis.

Quotations from the interviews will be included for illustrative purposes. A few quotations from published memoirs of past leaders of the Party will also be included. The interview quotations have been edited slightly to enhance clarity. Since the material was recorded and people do not speak in logical sequences (not even political leaders who have had long experience in public speaking) it was sometimes necessary to rearrange material. Words and meanings have not been changed, however. It can be a great temptation to the social scientist to add a final, summarizing line, or a poetic image to enhance the interest or the symmetry of the quotation. The temptation was resisted, as an examination of the transcriptions on file in the archives of the Columbia Oral History Collection will verify.

Punctuation has been substituted for oral and visual clues—a raised voice or a gesture—which, unfortunately, could not otherwise be indicated. The leaders are, without exception, individuals who have been very intensely committed to certain values and goals. The tones of outrage, impatience, anger, or frustration which frequently appeared in the interviews do not come through in the typescripts. Techniques such as italicizing and the use of exclamation marks are the only means available to convey these feeling tones.

This inquiry into the lives and times of three generations of political dissenters should be regarded as suggestive rather than definitive. The material presented here may evoke certain hypotheses that could be tested out on a broader, more quantitatively rigorous scale by other investigators in the future. For the general reader there will be an opportunity to enter, for a short while, one of the multiple worlds of meaning and belief that coexist in contemporary, complex, industrial societies.

CHAPTER I

SELF-IMAGES

BEFORE turning to an analysis of the life experiences of the leaders and their ideas about socialism, it would be instructive to get some notion of how they view themselves and, incidentally, of the kind of people who were attracted to and became leaders of the Socialist Party in this country.

While psychological differences are quite apparent, certain recurring self-images emerge which seem to override individual differences. Most of these self-images are strikingly consistent in all generations despite differences in salience and intensity of particular images in the three generations.

As I pointed out in the Introduction, almost all of the leaders continue to define themselves as socialists. Some have been out of the Party for thirty, forty, or even fifty years. What then does this persisting self-identification as a socialist consist of? One ex-leader, a labor union official who has been out of the Party since the 1930s replies:

Now, when you ask, "Are you still a socialist?" I believe in labor political action. I've always believed in it. What difference does it make whether I believe in political action in the form of a party or in the form of a force. That's nuts and bolts to me. That's a question of ways and means; it's not a question of principle.

Do I believe in the concept of social responsibility? Does society have a role in the economy and in protecting the lives of people? Yes! What else makes up socialism?

Two things are revealed in this quotation: an interest in people, their problems and needs, and a vague definition of socialism. A humanistic orientation is a central fact of existence in the lives of the leaders, whatever their present party affiliations or political activities may be.

The self-characterization as a socialist, for many of them, no longer seems to consist primarily of a belief in concrete, immediate, or ultimate economic and political goals which distinguishes socialists from other people. Their present goals vary greatly, from a desire for government ownership or control of basic industries to vague notions of increased social responsibility for the welfare of the citizenry. What seems to survive and constitute the identity, in addition to a belief in rather varied social goals, are certain humanistic values and qualities of character which they tend to attribute to themselves and to other socialists of the non-communist left:

A lot of my time was spent trying to recruit people into the socialist movement. You know, I would go to a party and I would be interested in finding other socialists. And if I met somebody who was decent—you know, who was bright and sensitive, I would say to myself, "He must be a socialist. Basically, he's *got* to be a socialist. He's bright and he's sensitive." And by the way, lots of times, they were.

And I was really a fervent man. After a while in New York, I decided to go to Chicago and be active recruiting people. And that's where I went. I went there in the summer of '57, I guess. Or '58, I don't know.

Anyway, in Chicago I had a marvelous time. I recruited dozens of people from the campus. Well, not dozens. That's an exaggeration. I recruited only a few people, but they were very good people.

They were all people who were in sensitive social milieus who were connected with other groups of people. They were young. They were active. They were interested in activity. They were bright. And they seemed to be pretty decent people, morally. So, I recruited them. And they were snap-doozers!

The leaders tend to view themselves as idealistic and dedicated, highly ethical and sensitive, and flexible and tolerant. Another core factor in their identity is intellectualism.

There is a feeling of community, of belonging together, which they feel toward all socialists, and which is less fragile now that differences of opinion regarding strategies and goals have become relatively meaningless in terms of possible effects on political institutions in the United States in the 1960s:

> The interesting thing is that as the radical movement has dwindled, non-communist left movements have tended to come a little closer to each other—at least in terms of sharing a common wailing wall.
>
> I remember back in the early 1930s formal debates between the YPSLs° and the anarchists. I would be the spokesman for the YPSLs against the head of the Young Anarchist League, or whatever its name was.
>
> A lot of the youngsters in those days—I shouldn't say a lot, but many of those that I debated—I now encounter in other relationships.
>
> And, of course, they've gone through evolutionary changes in their thinking too. They would no longer classify themselves as anarchists. They favor all kinds of government proposals. They favor the war against poverty program, and so on.
>
> There's a kind of cordiality that exists now although, in those days, there were very abusive exchanges.

Also, the community of self-identified socialists is believed by many respondents to extend well beyond the confines of the Socialist Party. They do not feel as alone as the present size of the Party would indicate:

> There is this very odd business where there is a kind of current revival of socialism. I mean, you find all sorts of strange people saying they're socialists. It's intellectually fashionable again to be a socialist. People who for many years, maybe, would say it privately, but never publicly, now, all of a sudden, are saying they're socialists.
>
> But to bring these people into a common organization and do something with this feeling is, perhaps, the problem that the Party faces—or the problem that socialists face.

Lifelong friendships formed initially in the Party are maintained on the basis of common values which persist long after the bases of common action have disappeared.

° Young People's Socialist League—youth organization of the Socialist Party.

My closest friends are not members of the Socialist Party now. They didn't lose their ideology. They lost their affiliation. They lost heart and their desire to be affiliated.

But this didn't affect personal friendships. There are common values that we have.

It's just a matter of their cheating us out of their services.

The feeling of community, of belonging together, and of sharing a common identity is strong and enduring for these leaders and ex-leaders. One has the feeling that their political identity is a crucial aspect of their self-identity, and that to deny this identity, however vague and segmented it may have become over the years, would be to deny their total existence as human beings.

IDEALISM

Idealism, as I shall use the term, refers to a belief in man's virtually unlimited potentialities for achieving humanistic goals— goals having to do with the satisfaction of human needs, material and nonmaterial.

The view of the self as idealistic emerges spontaneously and frequently in the interviews. The World War I Generation, however, is most unhesitating, uninhibited, and unguarded in affirming their idealism. Their high hopes remain relatively unimpaired, and the idealism of some of the leaders is almost unbounded. A ninety-year-old retired labor union official, who has been out of the Party since 1917, sees an unlimited future for mankind and for socialists:

A liberal may have as his objective a certain achievement. When it is achieved, there is no more. But the socialists have more to fight for, and the more may take a very long time. It makes no difference.

The socialist says, "I carry my message to the people. To the extent that the people accept it, I've done that much good. And if they accept that much, I'll carry the rest of the message."

And, inasmuch as in a free country there is no end to what progressive people may reach out for, as people advance, as countries advance, as thinking advances, there will always be room for a Socialist Party. That's the way I look at it.

Idealism is a matter of pride for this generation. They not only affirm their past idealism freely, they reaffirm their present idealism:

I think we all had the same vision: that we, the society, the people, all people, would have a chance to live in decency. We had a vision that justice and freedom and everything else would be there, under socialism, and that your job was to help bring it about. And you did what you could.

In 1912, I think it was, when Debs got a million votes, we all thought that socialism was around the corner. And when Victor Berger and Meyer London were elected to Congress, hopes were high.

Hopes are high when you are younger. You do your share in learning and sharing whatever knowledge you have with the masses on the street corners. There was no radio or television in those days, remember, and what we had to do was take a soap box and an American flag and preach the Gospel to anyone who would listen.

And they listened! I don't think they believed in what we preached, but they listened. And, occasionally, some of us quite often, would get a very satisfactory response—people asking questions and we giving them an answer. It was very exciting and very satisfying. . . .

We still have the dream, you know—for a better world. We all do. We still have a dream of a world without war, without poverty, without this, that, and the other thing that is obnoxious to our senses.

Very few leaders, only two, still believe that socialism, traditionally defined as government ownership of productive property, is inevitable. As one might guess, both of these leaders are in the World War I Generation. Others in this generation believe that socialism in its nonmaterial aspect, as a system of ethics, will inevitably gain acceptance in the world:

This, I think is something that only an older person can give you because this was how we grew up.

Human beings were thought of as human beings, not as people to be bought and sold, their labor power exploited—scrapped when they were no longer any good.

The idea of equalitarianism, equality among men, is the idealistic factor which was present when we used the word comrade. It was the fellowship of people who were linked together by the solidarity of suffering, a common exploitation which they were resolved to end.

You did not hate the capitalists as individuals, but you hated the system for which they stood, because you didn't think the interests of people and of profit could be finally reconciled.

With modern welfare state capitalism, you do not have the religion based on protest; based on a very deep conviction that you are being exploited.

This was the movement behind the Socialist Party. This was the feeling of agitation and protest. We lived strikes. We lived solidarity. We lived in a movement in which you gave, irrespective of what you hoped to get at some future time.

And you stood for people. You didn't stand for the dollar. You stood for the human being. That was the basic idea—the idealistic view—which will still come, maybe not under the name of socialism. But people will still be driven back to it, eventually, and in *that* way.

There is a persistence of the Marxist argot in this World War I generation: comrade, labor power, solidarity, exploitation, bourgeoisie, and proletariat. There is also a persistence of the religious metaphor: "We preached the Gospel." The younger generations rarely use this language and imagery.

When disillusionment is expressed in this generation, and it is rarely expressed, it is followed by a reaffirmation of earlier ideals. A leader who is in his eighties and still active in the Socialist Party, emphasizes optimism and inevitability:

I don't believe in the saying that you can't change human nature. If you mean by that, that you can't change human conduct under very different social conditions, I think you can!

But way down deep there are, in mankind, traits that aren't going to be eliminated. The love of power, I'm inclined to think, in my old age, is more serious than the love of profit. And if you get the power, you get the profits, you know.

You can see that in Russia. You can see it everywhere. The faults of man go deeper than I used to think.

But:

Socialism isn't going to die. And the name isn't even going to die. And it shouldn't die, because even if your means are not revolutionary, in the sense of breaking everything up, the goal has to be that there has to be planning to manage the world, in terms of production for the common good. And there will have to be increasing degrees of fairness in the distribution of whatever is produced. If you can't get constructive evolution, you'll get sabotage.

I don't believe in any far off or near-at-hand divine event toward which the whole creation inexorably inclines. This little experiment on earth can blow up. But it doesn't have to. At least there is nothing that anybody knows about that makes it inevitable. Therefore, we do our damndest, so to speak. And lots of things *do* get done.

Another leader in his eighties who is still politically active, after tracing in detail his defeats and disappointments, closes the interview with a final prediction:

The old movement of the classless and warless world is the kind of thing that we have to have and that we are *going* to have, if we are going to exist at all.

An indication of the persistence of idealism in this group is the fact that almost all of the leaders who emphasize the ethical and nonmaterial aspects of socialism, in their present conception of socialism, are members of this generation.

Changing fashions in idealism, and certainly in the expression of idealism, are indicated by the contrast between this generation and the Interwar Generation. While the Interwar Generation also tends to characterize itself as idealistic, the verbalization of idealism is less frequent, less impassioned, often parenthetical, and almost perfunctory:

I still have not only my old friends but I have my old ideals and my old concepts. And my new ways of working for them.

Or:

The goal is always the same. It is the freedom of the individual to achieve his potential creativity in fellowship with his fellow man.

There are few elaborations on this theme; no millennial predictions. This generation continues its work, primarily in nonprofit, special interest organizations, but its idealism is tempered by a narrowing of expectations:

People's demands are less than any of the old, ambitious ideologies would accept. People will settle for less.

And there is a narrowing of goals:

It started with an initial interest in problems, a concern for people, a concern for bettering the lot of individuals—very, very vague, very emotional, perhaps, very immature; but it was, I think, a very good feeling toward people and toward helping people. . . .

And the work I'm doing at the moment bears a relationship you know. Who's to argue that helping one person isn't as good as trying to save a hundred, or not being able to save a hundred thousand. So even what I'm doing today is, in part, related—working in social service.

Disillusionment runs very deep for some members of this generation. It extends not only to politics, but to people—old friends as well as old foes—who left the Party, as well as people who remained in the Party. Frustration cannot be categorically attributed to this evil or that strategy any more, and the failure of the Party, when it is accepted, is not readily explained. Disenchantment with old goals and old friends is particularly prominent in the Interwar Generation:

We accept the same welfarism that the other countries do—when and where we have to. Once medical costs begin to go up and decent medical treatment becomes impossible, especially for an older section of the population that now lives longer, we're ready to accept welfarism. Once you have a large section of the population in older cities with no place to live, there is no solution except welfarism.

If the wages in other countries were as high as the American wage for a large sector of the population, they also wouldn't accept welfarism. The tendency is, that if you can do for yourself, in a democratic society, you do! And you are reluctant to accept the group approach, except where you *cannot* do.

I know many people who subscribe to HIP°° for example. HIP is a terrific medical service. It's overall coverage. *But* you don't have as wide a choice as you'd like to have, very often. And there is a kind of

°° Health Insurance Plan

impersonality in the service that you get. The doctor *has* a big work load and he can't sit for an hour and talk to you.

So, I've noticed something. All my old socialist friends go for HIP and the rest of it. But when they can afford better, and they have a little unfortunate experience. they go *private*. They go buy themselves a doctor! They hold onto HIP because of the expensive lab tests and examinations. So it pays.

It's interesting to watch, because these are people who are ideologically convinced that the collective approach is better, that you get more for less, that it's socially desirable—all of that, all of that—and yet, where they can do it on their own, they tend to supplement the service by going on their own.

But, of course, when you can't, you stay with the collective approach. And maybe there is a certain amount of logic to this. You know, its an old cliché, of course, you do for yourself what you can, and what you can't do for yourself, you try to do collectively.

The leaders in the Interwar Generation tend to have the feeling of being a particularly ill-fated generation in the sense of having been in their political prime during a period of extraordinarily disabusing experiences and occurrences in the United States and in Europe:

The apocalyptic attitude toward the future is gone. As a personal factor, most people have lost it. And, I think, as an ideological or intellectual factor, it's almost indefensible.

I think the most important dimension of this type of thinking was that you can take a society, a very complex society which, in part, is highly differentiated and which lives by tradition, in some respects, and with very complicated relationships—that you can take a society like that and, with one fell swoop, turn it around and write a blueprint for a new society.

There's a very simple kind of rationalism there which, in part, goes very far back. It goes back to the eighteenth century—the belief that somehow you can cut society off, root and branch, and then simply, you know, rewrite it. I don't think that's true.

It's not true, it seems to me, as empirical sociological fact. It's not true, it seems to me, as a possibility in history. A lot of people have held that idea, and perhaps some people still do.

But I think that aspect of it is lost at least in the *older* generation. I think, after all, a generation which has gone through an experience of seeing concentration camps, betrayals, and terror, is not as sanguine about human nature and about mass movements, unrestrained, as younger people might be.

There's no notion any longer of the inherent goodness of man, in *any* respect. This, I think, at least for a certain generation, is gone— and, I think, quite rightly so.

This generation affirms its idealism in muted tones, and it is far less sanguine in its expectations regarding ultimate goals, when it still retains these goals, than the World War I Generation:

I really don't anticipate the kind of social ownership of industry that I believe in, in the United States. . . . And I must say, that if I didn't have such a strong philosophical commitment, such a strong belief that there is almost an immorality in private employment, as such, as a system, I suppose I could say: "Really, in comparison to the alternatives we see around us, in other countries, haven't we done so much better? Why should we care?"

Providing we proceed now with the things that we're headed to-wards, in relation to welfare, in relation to the minimum wage, and— now I have new hope—in relation to the spread of unionism into areas where it hasn't existed before: agriculture, the professions, and white collar work, etc. . . .

Really, we may end up with a sufficiently livable result, so that you could say, "O.K., I want to perfect it. I believe ideally it should be thus and so." And I really believe it. But I can see that this is an acceptable way of going on living.

The difference in the readiness of verbalize idealism and in the ultimate expectations of these two generations probably relates to age as well as to life experiences. With regard to life experiences, it must be remembered that the World War I Generation spent its most formative years in the Party, in an era of high expecta-tions both for humanity and for the Party.

The oldest respondents entered the Party at a time when many socialists expected that the Socialist Party would eventually achieve political power in this country:

In those years, from 1900 to 1904, there was a great deal of activity in the movement and a great hope that the movement would advance very rapidly.

The Socialist Party was officially organized in 1901, and from 1900 to 1904 the Socialist Party grew very rapidly, the vote of E. V. Debs having quadrupled from 100,000 to about 400,000.

A number of people in the Party at that time calculated that if the vote quadrupled from 1900 and 1904, and then quadrupled from 1904 to 1908 and from 1908 to 1912, socialism would perhaps be achieved in this country within a couple of decades.

Perhaps the greater optimism of this generation indicates the persistence of early, formative, political experiences in the lives of people. Early ways of thought have a tendency to become habitual.

Also, there is some evidence that optimism about the past may be a characteristic feature of old age. A recent nationwide survey of persons aged sixty-five and over in America, revealed an "unwavering optimistic set about the quality of past life experiences." [1]

Perhaps a compensating optimism sets in for the aged in modern industrial society in the face of the greatly attenuated authority and prestige that they experience. They are no longer the repository of ancient and venerable oral traditions and knowledge as they were in non-literate societies, and they are no longer in control of the economic resources of the more-or-less extended family as they were, usually, until their death in traditional, agricultural societies.

Despite recent evidence that the status of the aged probably never was uniformly high and was related to whether or not they relinquished control of political, economic, religious, and familial functions to their middle-aged children,[2] the conditions of isola-

[1] Ethel Shanas, "Restriction of Life Space—Attitudes of Age Cohorts," unpublished paper presented at the 62nd annual meeting of the American Sociological Association, San Francisco, August, 1967.

[2] See for example, Ethel Shanas and Gordon F. Streib, eds., *Social Structure and the Family: Generational Relations* (Englewood Cliffs, New Jersey: Prentice Hall, 1965).

tion and enforced retirement at the age of sixty-five are peculiar
to the aged in urban industrial society.

The oldest leaders have continued to work when they have the
choice (as self-employed lawyers). Those who were salaried employees and were retired at the age of sixty-five sometimes express resentment over their involuntary retirement, but they are
now engaged in a variety of service-oriented voluntary activities.
They keep busy, they are not isolated, and they are optimistic.
The belief that socialism did not fail, or will not fail, is most pre-
valent in this generation, as we shall see in Chapters III and IV.

A high degree of optimism was perhaps also characteristic of
the Interwar Generation up until the beginning of World War II:

I came to New York again in 1940. We moved campaign headquarters for the Party here. The National Office was still in Chicago,
but the Party campaign was run from New York.

I don't think that at that time we had given up the idea that
socialism would be successful in America. It's hard for me to read
back in, but it seems to me that we felt very strongly, at least up until
World War II, that we *were* going to win in the United States.

I am sure that was the feeling in the 1940 campaign. Not that we
were going to elect anybody in 1940, but as far we could see, capitalism was in collapse.

The Interwar Generation leaders, however, were leaders of the
Party when most of the disillusioning events touched upon in the
Introduction took place: the disillusionment with the working
class as an agency of radical change, the persistence of war, the
depression that was ended by World War II and not by rational
economic planning, the rise of totalitarianisms of the right and
the left, and the cynicism and debunking of the psychological era.
And they have not managed for the most part to maintain the
optimism of the World War I Generation.

They are also, it must be remembered, middle-aged—an age
which is often characterized, particularly in the middle class in
our society, by disenchantment, deprivation, and stress.

In a society in which the nuclear family is the characteristic
kinship unit, socially, economically, and residentially, the break-

ing of ties with children is a typical deprivation of middle age. Conflicts between middle-aged parents and their adolescent children are more profound, not only because of rapid social change, which outmodes the values and attitudes of parents to a greater extent than in the past, but because relationships are more intense in nuclear families. There are fewer children and often no unattached maiden aunts or bachelor uncles or grandparents to mediate the conflicts between parent and child.

The middle-aged experience a loss of youth (in a society where youth is very highly valued), lowered strength and vitality, and possible ill-health. In their most productive years, they often endure the stress of supporting two dependent generations—the young and the old—who, in modern, industrial society, remain outside of the productive process.

Finally, there is a typical disenchantment which sets in at middle age, particularly for the achievement-oriented middle class. It is the spokesman for the middle-aged in our society who originally coined the cliché, "the moment of truth" to refer to the sudden realization that youthful dreams of glory will never materialize. The belief in the possibility of achieving certain goals—fame, fortune, love, happiness—can be maintained by the young. Time is on their side. In our society, the realization dawns in middle age that certain if not many goals will never be attained. This may be an additional factor in the pervading tone of disillusionment in this generation: "Youth has fled; their best years have been passed in the service of the Party or of the ideal. They are aging, and with the passing of youth, their ideals have also passed, dispersed by the contrarieties of daily struggles, often, too, expelled by newly acquired experiences which conflict with the old beliefs." [3]

In contrast to the World War I Generation, only a few of the respondents in the Interwar Generation are still active in the Socialist Party. Considering their younger median age (fifty years), this is a further indication of their greater disillusionment.

[3] Robert Michels, *Political Parties* (Glencoe, Illinois: The Free Press, 1949), p. 221. This book was first published in 1915.

The World War II Generation also views itself as idealistic, but this idealism must be inferred largely from their statements of their dedication to the Party and the time and energy that they have spent on Party activities.

The leaders in this generation tend to avoid specific expressions of idealism. They do not predict ultimate attainments for mankind, and they make quite clear their unwillingness to do so. Visions of a classless and warless world are completely outside of their perspective. Their idealism is far more constricted than that of the World War I Generation, or even the Interwar Generation.

Expectations were never high, and disenchantment, therefore, is not a recurring theme, as it is for the Interwar Generation. A writer who joined the Party in 1944 describes the horizons of this generation:

By the time I came into contact with the Party, it was not at its height. I suppose it had more of a past than a future.

What kept me involved in it was the idea that socialist ideas and ideals and concepts should at least be presented and have an audience. And, up to the extent that we could, we tried to maintain that.

It wasn't a matter of feeling that the socialist movement was going to make a great impact, at the time that I was in it, but simply that socialist ideas should at least be kept relevant and kept before the public.

We felt we should engage in what today we call a dialogue. There was always this constant hope that we would force our way into, or be invited to discuss things with groups who were closest to the periphery of the Democratic Party, politically, or to the general intellectual community, so that they would be concerned about socialist goals, socialist thinking, socialist analysis.

I think this is about as far as one could say we hoped we might go in this period in terms of sheer impact. And this was true also of the fifties.

And, well, it's still true.

This generation tends to view itself as more pragmatic than the leaders in the World War I Generation and in the Interwar Generation who are still active in the Party. A major issue within the Party at present is over the question of whether or not socialists should actively work within the Democratic Party, in their identity as socialists, to slough off the more conservative elements in the Democratic Party and to realign it in a more radical direction. The goal of these socialists is to achieve something like the equivalent of the British Labour Party in the United States. While the top leadership of the Socialist Party is in favor of realignment, as this position is called, there is a generational conflict on this issue.

For the youngest generation, a realignment position is not in conflict with their idealism. Political effectiveness is an overriding value. There is respect for the older members of the Party:

What has happened is that the dominant political position within the Party—or tendency, whatever you want to call it—is not one that I feel particularly happy with.

One has to admire them, because they are, in a sense, keeping the Socialist Party alive, and so on. But on the other hand, they just are not in tune with the political realities of America in 1965.

But:

I'm not for going in again with one foot on cloud nine. Every day of the year, concrete political problems arise. I'm not only concerned with my long-range socialist goals. I'm also concerned with everyday issues that arise.

I'm concerned with questions like the civil rights bill that was just adopted, and whether or not it was going to include an amendment outlawing the poll tax or not. I'm interested in the whole question of the war on poverty and how it's going to be conducted—whether it's going to be a real war on poverty, or whether it's going to be phony war on poverty.

I'm interested in every social, political, and economic issue that faces the American people, and I need an instrument for being effective on those things. I want to have my rights as a citizen as much as any Republican or Democrat.

The fact that I'm a socialist doesn't mean that I'm satisfied to say, "I'm for the socialist ideal, the socialist form of society, and I don't care what goes on in the world around me."

I do care, *very, very* much. And I don't see how any socialist can help but care. And I want to have—I *need* to have, I think all socialists need to have—avenues of being effective politically, as effective as any other citizen in the day-to-day problems that arise in American politics.

The Socialist Party is obviously not such an avenue. In the Socialist Party you cannot effect these things. And I don't want to be merely a letter writer, although I'm for writing letters to Congressmen.

I want to have something to say about whether the Congressman in my district is going to be a hack or a reactionary or a really authentic, genuine liberal. The liberal is not a socialist, but he's far preferable, from a socialist standpoint, to the hack or to the reactionary.

And I don't think socialists can or ought to take the attitude that it doesn't make any difference to us. And that's another reason why I think that socialists ought to be involved in the Democratic Party.

An all-embracing idealism and ideology is in fact conceived of as a handicap by the youngest members of this generation:

Listen, let me tell you something. The socialist movement is the sickest when it starts replacing all other institutions in life. That's the surest sign that there's going to be a terrible factional fight tomorrow.

You know, when it starts becoming a combination moral, religious, and political organization—forget about it. That's a disaster.

Look, the thing you have to remember about it is that the Socialist Party is only one thing. It's a political organization—the expression of certain ideas, certain general ideas about how society ought to be organized. Because it's a political organization, it does not involve people feeling superior to the rest of humanity. Once you start thinking, gee whiz, this is my moral fervor here, you know, then what you're really doing is, you're saying, "I'm superior to other people." You see? Then you start having that inward orientation, as opposed to the outward orientation.

What you have to have is an organization that looks towards politics, towards doing things on the outside. Once it starts doing that, once it starts effectuating other things, then it's possible for people to express themselves politically through the organization, you see.

Now, some people will find a very meaningful thing in that, because they're political people. That's a healthy relationship to politics, you see. You want to be politically active because you're a socialist and the socialist movement is doing things in these fields that you're involved in or that you want to be involved in.

And this is a new way for you to coordinate your activity with other people around the country so that you're all in connection with one another. That's healthy. But when you think of replacing it, of replacing your whole life structure with the movement, as often happens, that's disastrous. That's unhealthy. It's like a fever.

The dramatic contrast between the generations is indicated by the following statement of the role of idealism and ideology in the life of a World War I Generation leader who joined the Party in the early 1900s:

You have to live through it. It was like a religion. It was like an inspiration. It was like a commitment. Just as a missionary goes out and preaches to the heathen in foreign countries, so we socialists got on soap boxes and persuaded people that industry could be run for use and not for profit.

The thing we emphasized was not the money a man had, but Ruskin's idea, "There is no wealth but life, life with all its capacities for love, joy, pleasure, and recreation."

A woman who went to work in the garment industry in 1908, at the age of eleven, recalls the meaning of the Party and the ideology in her life:

Probably, if I had to live my life all over again, I'd do the same thing, you know. It was a satisfaction. It was a hope. It was a goal. It was a vision. It was a dream. . . .

You shed light on certain matters. You awakened people's consciousness to their own situation. You gave meaning to life. . . . You gave meaning to the long hours and the low wages and the horrible living conditions.

When you were cold, you were warmed by the idea that someday it was going to be better. When you were hungry, you were cheered because someday the Union was going to see to it that you earned a decent living. When you were lonely, you had your comrades there.

It really was something worthwhile. No question about it. It was something to work for. Something that kept you thinking. It kept your mind working—the lectures you went to, the meetings you attended, the people you saw. Not only for me, but for numberless people I know, it was a relief and a release from boredom, monotony, almost hopelessness, in what you were doing.

The organization you belonged to gave you hope, and gave you fortitude, and gave you something to think about and to like and to read. You realized that you had a mind of your own, and that you would like to cultivate it.

And if you couldn't go to school, you had to do it yourself, on your own. And you did it, together with comrades, and in a way that was really quite enjoyable.

The fringe benefits of idealism are not as available to the youngest leaders. Perhaps it is time to reevaluate present, possibly anachronistic, stereotypes of youthful idealism. Young people may continue to brave the paths of untried heroism but, in the present era of foreshortened visions, this may be more a function of a belief in youthful omnipotence than an unquestioning belief in the human potential for rationalism.

DEDICATION

The leaders also view themselves as dedicated people, willing to sacrifice personal gain or comfort for social goals. The means have become increasingly educational rather than political, as I indicated in the Introduction, when we noted the occupational shift in the World War II Generation away from work in nonprofit interest organizations. The renunciation of materialism and an intense commitment to social goals, however defined or redefined, is a common motif in the interviews.

It must be remembered that our respondents have all been, or are, leaders of the Party. The Party was, or is still to some extent, the core of their existence. They lived, breathed, worked for, and married in the Party. Statements such as "It embraced my life" and "It became the entire focus of my life" and "It absorbed all my energies" are typical in describing their relationship to the Party at the height of their leadership.

Disapproval of the business ethic and emphasis on service to the community is a recurrent theme. Only one of the thirty-four respondents is engaged in a business occupation—and he is a writer. The choice of work in nonprofit service activities is the only conceivable one for some leaders:

My approach, after a very short period of romanticism when I first joined, was that I was going to spend my life working for socialism and for unionism, civil rights, and such causes.

I had made up my mind that this was the only life that was worth living, and that this was what I would do. And while the economic circumstances of my life have changed from what I originally thought they were going to be, it really doesn't matter too much.

Up until the time that we started having a family, I worked for the Socialist Party. Let me put it this way: I had been an organizer of the Socialist Party in Chicago up to 1942, and at that time I was getting something like forty-five dollars a week.

Then I was asked to come to the national office in New York as National Secretary. And the national office was in bad shape. All it could pay was thirty-five dollars a week, which it did, and which eventually went up to forty-five dollars.

But it wasn't until we were ready to start a family, and my wife was pregnant, that I said to the Executive Committee, rather sheepishly, that I would now have to have seventy-five dollars a week.

It never dawned on me before that it was necessary to have money. As long as we had enough money to have an apartment and to eat, and so on, that was the important thing.

Yet, I never had a feeling of deprivation, because I was doing the things that I considered important and worthwhile. I never felt that I was sacrificing for the movement.

My reaction was that people who found making money an important part of life—this I found weird. And I still do. This doesn't mean that I don't like money and the things it can buy. I do. But I just can't conceive of this as a basis for working. I couldn't take a job I didn't like and believe in. And I'm very fortunate in that, except for a couple of factory jobs that I had in my youth, all the jobs I have had have been ones that I really felt useful in and enjoyed.

For other leaders, other possibilities are conceivable. There is ambivalence and, perhaps, rationalization. But it was, and is, a matter of choice:

Personally, there's no question that it was a matter of choice. I mean, it's embarrassing to say, you know, "I could have done this." And some of it would be silly.

But there's no question, knowing my own abilities, and I say this immodestly, that in each of the following directions I could have done fairly well (they're not related to each other): one is in the mathematics and logic field, which is really a primary interest of mine and almost predates my politics, early as that may have been. Although I was not much of a student, as a student I was teaching logic in college, for example.

No question about the law field which comes to me so easily. And that's one thing I do regret. I think I could have done most of what I did anyway, have taken a law degree, and solved a lot of my financial problems that way.

It happens that my actual academic work was in economics where I don't really think I have a lot of ability, except in certain mathematical aspects of it.

Also, again, very immodestly, I think I am a very outstanding teacher and discussion leader. Nowadays, for a little over a year, I have been running a weekly radio program. I don't give it over half hour's attention except the half hour I spend on the program. And it's very successful—gets featured listings in almost all the daily newspapers every week.

On top of all that the field which I will probably go into some day when I retire is stock market speculation. I am a very effective stock market speculator. And *that* is, no question about it, the easiest way to make a living that there is around. And it's not uninteresting to me. I find it very amusing. And it does involve my economics and my mathematics and even a bit of my understanding of public opinion.

But this leader has reached his moment of truth:

Today I might not make the choice I made. This year I'll be fifty. And if I weren't so deeply committed to my particular job and a particular set of accomplishments I have there, it is possible that I would decide to change.

Social position colors perception. The only leader among our respondents who left the Party in the 1930s to become a business man does not view dedication to socialist ideas and work in non-profit interest organizations as a matter of choice except for a few, and he feels, furthermore, that Socialist Party goals have been achieved:

Only the least able and the least energetic followed their fathers into the movement and into the unions—but in a different classification, not as workers. Many of them became organizers in the trade unions and the craft unions.

Then some were attracted to communism as a solution, but it didn't have much appeal actually until the 1930s, and then its appeal was simply that of desperation.

The solution was provided for the great majority—now I'm not talking about certain Jewish intellectuals—by what might be called the adoption of the Socialist Party platform by the Democratic Party under Roosevelt, which, if you examine it, is programmatically about the same thing.

The country becomes responsible for your welfare if you can't have a job. It goes through all the formulations which are actually oriented toward socialist thinking and derived from socialist experiment and socialist theory.

A goal abandoned is a goal achieved. We will come back to the phenomenon of the displacement of goals later in our analysis when we discuss our respondents' present conceptions of socialism.

MORALITY

In a period of prosperity, the welfare state, supersonic rates of change, the blurring of meanings, and the redefining and over-lapping of goals of the different classes, the class struggle thesis of the socialist movement does not have as much appeal as it did in the days of unregulated capitalism.

Intellectuals have substituted the concepts of status and inter-est groups for that of class in their analyses of contemporary society. Socialists, increasingly, have tended to redefine socialism as a set of ethical principles embodying humanistic goals: "Social-ism, in practice, has become a very pragmatic affair, but it com-monly emphasizes, especially since World War II, its ethical aspect." [4]

A young leader, currently quite active in the Socialist Party,

[4] Norman Thomas, *Socialism Re-examined* p. 29.

emphasizes the shift in orientation from class to ethics: "Most people who come into the radical movement don't have a class. They have a conception of morality."

Our respondents consider themselves highly ethical people. This comes through directly:

I think morality in the United States is in a state of collapse. . . . Our traditional morality, you know, for good or evil, is dying.

And there are lots of things about the old morality that I like. There's a certain austerity in the Puritan tradition that I like.

I think that a certain kind of purity, of Puritanism, is excellent—absolutely excellent!

Or, it comes through indirectly, in criticisms of the corruption, materialistic values, and brutality in American society:

Basically, one doesn't like a society with the contrasts of wealth and poverty and with recurrent wars, and so on—a society with all the brutality that characterized and characterizes our society.

. . .

We have a society now which is obviously capable of filling all of the needs, not only of the American people, but of half the people of the world—and which is failing so miserably to do it.

Of course, it can always give more automobiles. But even the things it gives are geared so obviously to selling products which people don't even need, and not meeting all kinds of other needs.

People are driving around in Cadillacs and their kids are illiterate. I used to work in a factory in Jersey for about five years, and guys would come to work driving a Cadillac and then go home and there was no food in the icebox. And they were living in two rooms with no heat, you know.

The values are so corrupted, and so obviously so, from the point of view of what's going to be most profitable—much more so than at an earlier period.

Our respondents view the socialist movement, with the exception of the communist left, as a highly ethical movement:

The value system of the socialist movement, the kind of things that are our pride, you know, are the kind of things that are the best of America—the idea of civil liberties, the idea of social justice, the idea

of people being intrinsically important, and not just important as
consumers, you know, or as workers.

They view the Party as highly ethical:

The original motivation to join was, of course, a highly moral motivation. You came in with a great sense of Party. You came in with a
great sense of pride. You came in with a great sense of devoting your
life to something which is pure and important.

And they view the late Norman Thomas, leader and symbol of
the Party, as highly ethical:

That's why Thomas has come off so well. Thomas' ideas are not so
impressive, you know—compared to the rest of the socialist movement. He's not an independent thinker, particularly.

But he has tremendous moral stature which he has earned over the
years. And that kind of thing is decisive. You can't replace that. You
can replace almost anything else. But not that.

A World War I Generation leader uses the religious metaphor:

Norman Thomas is a man of impeccable personal character—a sort of
secular saint.

But for one Interwar Generation leader, Norman Thomas'
morality has been a disadvantage to the Party:

Thomas, in my opinion, whom I have always regarded as a great
personal figure, a personal leader—I think Thomas has had a big hand
in pulling the socialist movement away from any possibility of becoming a mass movement.

He never wanted to appeal to the mass. He always wanted to be an
upholder of Truth, not the developer of mass sentiment for social
change.

He was a moral leader. I don't mean to say that one should be an
immoral leader. I mean that one should make adjustments. For example, in the Old-Guard-Militant fight when the Old Guard split off
from the Party in the thirties, even *there* was a moment when Norman
said, "The question isn't what is in the interests of the goals we're
headed toward. The question is, who's right and who's wrong?"

This is the way it always was with Norman. And that's because
Norman was always the spokesman for—some people call it the Chris-

tian socialists. Well, it could be Jewish just as easily as Christian. That isn't the point.

The concept that his role is a moral one—the conscience of the community, you know—that's his great success, his great victory, as well as his defeat.

Instead, he should have said—and this is because I'm a Marxist: "My role is to organize those healthy drives which motivate a large mass of people for self-interest reasons and which lead in the direction of society's welfare. To mobilize this so as to win these things." This was the basis of the successful European Socialist Parties. They said, "We are here to mobilize. . . ."

For another leader, the morality of the European non-communist socialist movement has been *its* undoing:

The Social Democratic Parties produced good people, but they were ineffective leaders. They couldn't use force in times of crisis.

For a few of our respondents, socialism represents a conscious transvaluation and a practical application of religious ethics which led to the original decision to join the Party:

We were a very religious family, and when I finally came across socialism, I thought that it was the kind of thing that I had been looking for—in terms of the Christian spirit.

The thing that actually made me a socialist, which I recognized when I found it, was the parable of the day laborer in the vineyard.

If you remember, they went out to work for different hours, but they all received for their work one penny. That was to me, an illustration of "From each according to his ability, to each according to his need."

I had that kind of perception of people in relation to money, that it was *people* who were important, and their needs, and not either the kind of work or the amount of work that they did.

. . .

I think the thing that prodded me most: it was an indirect process that took place and it stems basically from my religious interests.

I had decided when I was fourteen or fifteen, that I was going to become a reform rabbi. I was very much influenced by Rabbi Stephen Wise.

The chain is an odd one. Rabbi Wise had as a guest in his pulpit one day John Haynes Holmes from the Community Church. Holmes was very close to the Socialist Party, as you know. I became interested in Holmes as an orator, and I went to hear him preach at the Community Church.

Then, it must have been in the summer of 1924, I went down to the Community Church. I had been attending there regularly on Sunday mornings, more or less. And Norman Thomas occupied the pulpit one Sunday morning. And I became very interested.

There you have the specific links. My interest in religious-ethical concepts then started my thinking in terms of the political application of these ideas. My background was not a Marxian socialist background. And you couldn't call me a Christian socialist—maybe a Jewish socialist, in the religious sense.

Some leaders, who feel that the Socialist Party failed only in the political sense, emphasize the moral legacy which the Party left to this country:

I think that while the Socialist Party did fail, organizationally and politically, it didn't fail in that it always had a kind of moral stance which I think is very important and still, in many ways, conditions the thinking of a lot of people.

If you take what I regard to be the fundamental position of a socialist—I think the phrase is summed up by Tawney: that you don't like an acquisitive society. You don't like a society in which reward is unfair, and in which you have a system which, in part, maximizes unfair rewards. Or, you don't like one in which certain social needs take hind position.

That type of emphasis by and large, and for all sorts of reasons, has, in effect, taken hold much more strongly in American life and become a very important force of its own. With some it merges with the welfare state. With some it goes beyond that.

In a subtle and latent sense, the Socialist Party was an unmatched training ground for people to gain organizational skills, ideological skills, political skills.

Given the fact that these skills came into demand because of the nature of the War, and the fact that the American government under the New Deal was more receptive to these people—and the labor movement was growing—there were modes of access out of the Party into rather significant areas of American life.

So, I think if one were to look back at the Socialist Party, you'd probably find an extremely high proportion of people, not just leaders, but middle-level people, middle-echelon people, lower-rank leaders, who, one way or another, were able to move out into very important positions, particularly in universities, government, and the trade union movement. And they brought their values with them—in an attenuated form.

The point about ethics, however, is that the Judeo-Christian code of ethics appears to be on its way out in America. What Martha Wolfenstein [5] has called the "fun morality" is in. The Judeo-Christian ethic, insofar as it emphasized impulse denial and delayed gratification, served a useful function in production-oriented economies of scarcity. In secularized, rationalized, consumption-oriented economies, it becomes a hindrance, if not an irrelevance.

SENSITIVITY

Sensitivity to human suffering is implicit in much of the reminiscences of our respondents, but is not a dominant theme; possibly because it conflicts with the image of the political activist. In the World War II Generation it is verbalized directly:

I identify with the Negroes and I like to think I identify with all oppressed people. I've always been very sensitive in that way. I've always had a strong sense of social justice.

. . .

Look, I cannot live on 4th Street, off the Bowery, without becoming neurotic. I have to pass by alcoholics in the gutter.

Now, I either stop and take care of them, which is not possible unless I'm prepared to be a saint and give up my home. You see, I pass so many on one night, on the same night—on a summer's evening there will be one alcoholic to every doorway along 3rd Street. What

[5] Martha Wolfenstein, "Fun Morality: An Analysis of Recent American Child-Training Literature," in Margaret Mead and Martha Wolfenstein, eds., *Childhood in Contemporary Cultures* (Chicago: University of Chicago Press, 1955), pp. 168–78.

do I do? Do I take care of each one? How do I take care of them?
What do I do?

Well, confronted by this, you do nothing at all—nothing for any of
them. Because you can't help all of them, you help none of them. This
is incomprehensible, if you were born and raised with a feeling for
human beings.

In published memoirs by leaders of the Socialist Party who
were contemporaries of some of the World War I Generation
leaders in our study, sensitivity is expressed indirectly in recalling
the decision to join the Party.[6]

While the basic attraction of the movement was ideological,
the precipitating incident may have been an act of cruelty or
injustice, or the witnessing of the suffering of fellow workers:
militia firing at striking workers, the death of large numbers of
workers in a fire or an explosion, or an industrial accident to a
fellow worker: "That night and for many nights thereafter, I kept
thinking of Mary Bolan. Her right hand mutilated, made useless,
gone forever. Who would take care of Mary Bolan now? Owners
of factories wanted strong, healthy workers, workers with ten, not
eight fingers."[7]

One of our respondents describes a senseless act which for him
dramatically symbolized man's cruelty and man's vulnerability,
and led to his decision to join the Party:

In 1914 the soldiers were marching to the station. They had flowers
and they were singing. There was music and people were waving to
them. And I also waved. People were throwing flowers to the soldiers
—it was just the first week of the war. And one flower fell outside of
the line of marching troops. A young soldier took a step out of line to
pick up the flower. And the sergeant pushed him back in a way that,
for me, was disturbing and destroying.

I still have the young man in mind. I never saw him again. I'm sure
I will not see him again. But his face had changed immediately. There

[6] See, for example, Louis Waldman, *Labor Lawyer* (New York: E. P.
Dutton and Co., 1944); James Maurer, *It Can Be Done* (New York: Rand
School Press, 1938); and Bill Haywood, *Bill Haywood's Book* (New York:
International Publishers, 1929).

[7] Waldman, *Labor Lawyer,* p. 25.

was anxiety and the fear of death. Anxiety and the fear of shooting. Anxiety and the fear of what could happen. And a contempt for the sergeant which he could not express. The whole emotional scale was on his face.

And this changed everything for me. It was really incredible. I had never thought before that soldiers die. Or, if they die, they die in heroism, but not a common death with contempt for a sergeant, with fear and anxiety, and all of that.

I am sure the soldier was not married; he was too young. But he had a mother—or perhaps he did not have one, anymore. He had friends and girl friends. And his whole life was in an uproar at that moment. He was in the machinery of the army where he was nothing else any more than someone who is ordered around and pushed around by a sergeant.

And from then on, I started to be interested in socialism—to read everything. I joined the Party I believe, three years later, in 1917.

The sensitivity of the leaders is something which can best be described rather than illustrated: facial expressions, gestures, posture, and eye movements cannot be conveyed in quoted excerpts.

As a sociologist, I have interviewed other groups of people, in various settings for various purposes, and have never had the feeling as strongly, until these interviews, that it was absolutely essential to be as neutral as possible in the questioning and summarizing statements. I had an ever-present awareness that any sign of disagreement or disapproval, or the contrary, would be instantly recognized and responded to by the leaders.

The conversational exchanges in the interviews revealed and reflected the leaders' extraordinary perception of the purpose of the questions. They often anticipated, and usually correctly, what was about to be asked, and responded to what was meant by a question regardless of what was said.

FLEXIBILITY AND TOLERANCE

The leaders also believe they are flexible and tolerant people, that is, not authoritarian in their relationship with other human beings and not rigid or doctrinaire in their ideological views. This self-portrayal is implicit in the contrasts they draw between themselves and the communist left. Negative attitudes toward communism are expressed gratuitously, and often, by almost all of the leaders. The disapproval of communism centers on the authoritarianism of communists:

Money in our present-day society is necessary as a security. But the people who think that money in itself creates happiness, or a feeling of well-being and of usefulness, and of respect and love and comradeship and fellowship—which, after all, are the things that make life good or bad, their absence makes it bad, their presence makes life good— those things cannot be purchased by money.

That's the idea of the movement, along with the economics of Marx: surplus value, the buying of labor power, and so on. That was the economic basis. But on that, as anybody will tell you, there was the wide humanistic range. Nobody had a higher estimate of the capacities of the human race to rise above itself, so to speak, and build a decent world, than Marx did.

He lived in a humanistic age. People believed in that. They hadn't had the factual setback of fascism, showing that man could rise, but he could also fall.

And they hadn't had the communists coming along and taking one stray remark out of Marx's comments on the commune and switching it over to a whole philosophy, which they called the dictatorship of the proletariat.

What Marx envisaged as a possible emergency situation in which parliamentary methods were out, the Bolsheviks took and played up as their main creed. And it became the dictatorship not of the proletariat, but of the Party. And then it became the dictatorship of the communist clique, of the dominant person there, of the individual. And that fouled everything up. They spoke about socialism in those terms and they brought it into disrepute.

These are the things that the communists did to socialism with their dictatorship, and what Hitler did with his Nazi socialism. These are the things that have smeared, obscured, degraded, and stigmatized the concept of socialism.

Only one leader makes no reference to communism or the Communist Party at all in his reminiscenses, and no leader in any generation expresses a positive feeling toward the American Communist Party or to Soviet Communism. However, there is a tendency for negative attitudes to decrease in intensity and for neutral attitudes to increase in number in the younger generations. This undoubtedly reflects, in part, the decline in active conflict and competition between the Communist and Socialist Parties in this country in recent years, as the activities of both have become increasingly curtailed.

The younger leaders are impatient with sectarianism, dogmatism, and with the old issues: "I never want to hear the Russian Revolution mentioned again. I was sick of that whole approach years ago. Anyone who wants to discuss the American Revolution, good! But that whole European hangover of the movement has always been a bad influence."

In their initial contact with the socialist movement, some of our respondents were in doubt about which Party to join—the Socialist Party or the Communist Party. Further contact dispelled these doubts:

I really must say I think in this respect I'm atypical. I don't think my experience is the common thing. First of all, my age: I was born in 1934. That means that by the time I became interested and involved in politics, even hypothetically involved, it was way after the 1930s generation and the Second World War.

I guess I first became a socialist when I was about fourteen or fifteen years of age. I had no contact with the movement whatsoever. It was not a case of running across a socialist who was very persuasive, or any personal relationship whatsoever.

I started to read the novels of Upton Sinclair. This was in New York City. Upton Sinclair wrote this Lanny Budd series which was all about the adventures of a millionaire socialist.

I've looked back at them recently and they're sort of terrible novels. But Upton Sinclair always had a certain knack of raising your interest, and I became very interested.

In one of the books, Lanny Budd has a political discussion with an anarchist, I think, about politics. And he says, "Well, I can't be a capitalist because they make money out of the suffering of poor people, and so forth. And I can't be a fascist because they murder people, and communists murder people, so," he said, "I guess I'm a socialist."

Well, that was me. I thought about it and started to get interested in the socialists. I was thirteen or fourteen years old. And like many socialists, I guess—I don't even know if it's a general thing—I was a socialist, but I didn't know any other socialists. I didn't know any socialists at all!

Then I met a couple of communists when I was fifteen, or so, in a high school history class. One day I wasn't prepared, and the teacher asked a question—examples of cooperation of Americans with foreign groups before the Second World War. I used as an example the arms embargo to Spain.

Well, that was kind of an unusual thing for a high school kid of sixteen to bring up, and after the end of the class some guy walks up to me, a fellow student, and says, "Say, that's an interesting thing you brought up." He talks to me about it and asks me to come over that evening to a discussion group that a group of his friends had. I had no idea what was going on. But why not?

Later, when we got off the subway, he said to me as we were walking along in the Bronx, "I guess you should know that I'm a communist." I had no idea what a communist was, or a Shintoist, or anything else. I said, "Well, yes, of course, I assumed that," you know, playing the game.

Well, we went to his friend's apartment. I was very impressed because all of his friends were college people, and I was just a high school kid. They started talking about Korea. It was just the time of the Korean War. His friend started, and his first sentence was, "When South Korea invaded North Korea. . . ."

I said, "But I think North Korea invaded South Korea." And with that, we went off on two hours of debate: who invaded whom, geography, and one thing or another. Toward the end I got kind of tired and I said, "Look it doesn't make any difference. You can tell me that North Korea was provoked into it. Let's get on to something else."

But he refused to give up on this. It was as if the universe depended on this one idea, this one essential concept. If I didn't get that, I really couldn't be a good fellow.

Well, I refused to give in—I saw no reason to—and, as a result, they never asked me back. I suppose if they had been a little more flexible, I might have been more sympathetic to the communist movement in those early days.

But I was always aware that the communists murdered people. That was a sort of essential idea. It was not the idea that they murdered socialists so much, but just that they were killing people. And that was not my road.

Other leaders never had any doubt about which party to join:

Personally, I was never, never for one moment, attracted to the Communist Party—and I think this is more a personality thing, or maybe a bit of family background. To me, the concept of individual freedom, bordering on anarchism has always been the ideal.

And there was never a moment, even in the days—and I had many periods in which I worked in united fronts with the communists— when I felt that what they were saying made any sense, quite frankly.

Let me put it this way: I would say that always, from the earliest days in my life, I have been an anti-authoritarian. Always I looked on socialism not merely as the door that led to plenty, but as the door that led through plenty to complete individual freedom.

And, therefore, a movement which, in my opinion, to the knowledge of its participants (even though some may not have recognized it), really always said that it didn't believe in individual freedom, couldn't be going where I was going.

Several leaders recall that the initial choice was not a deliberate choice at all but, rather, a fortuitous event which they view in retrospect as a fortunate one:

I had doubts about society as it existed, and in high school, in the social problems club, which was a place for gathering in people like myself, there were one or two people who were connected with the Young People's Socialist League, the YPSLs.

This must have been in 1932 or something like that—'32 or '31. It was really in that club that I started to meet people. I met YPSLs and I met young communists who were attracted to the club. I really didn't know anything about the gradations and the difference between communists and socialists at that time.

One particular YPSL that I met invited me to YPSL meetings. I began to attend, and I found people of similar inclinations. It was an imperceptible process of being sucked in. My intentions certainly were not to join the Young People's Socialist League, or to enter the socialist movement.

Frankly, I don't think I knew what socialism was. I had very vague ideas at the time. As a matter of fact, if I were to analyze it, I would think that it was a rather utopian approach—about building a better world.

The differing methods and the problems and the difficulties of the communists vs. the socialists—these things weren't at all involved in my thinking. The YPSL was merely an organization that believed in a better world, and here I was going to become a part of it.

It was only after I was in the Party that I began to realize that there were different approaches and different problems and so on, in the different organizations. Now, maybe, there but for the grace of God (as the saying goes)—maybe if I had been attracted to a young communist, I could very well have gone that way.

I'm sure that if an analysis is done of people, of how they enter these movements—nobody sits down deliberately to think this thing through. I think once you've made your choice, you begin to rationalize your situation.

Probably this respondent's attraction to a young socialist rather than a young communist was not at all fortuitous, but was predetermined by values and attitudes which he recognizes were not as explicit and as conscious as they later became. That they became more precise and exact after joining the Party is due to the fact that a group which adheres to norms and values which differ from those of the dominant groups in the society must spell out these dissenting ways of thinking and acting, over and over again, for purposes of socialization and, above all, for reinforcement.

Within the Socialist Party, particularly since the Stalinist purges of the mid-1930s, the phrase democratic socialism has come into widespread use. The phrase is used to distinguish the socialism of the Socialist Party and its membership from that of the American Communist Party, the communism of the Soviet Union, and other totalitarian forms. The emphasis is on the word democratic:

One of the things that first caught my attention about socialism, in reading about it, was the simple statement that socialism is the application to our economic and social life of the political democracy that we enjoy in this country. It was the extension of this notion of democracy to an area where obviously it does not exist or has not existed.

It was this that attracted me intellectually to socialism, and it is this that makes it still an attractive idea to people. And it's the thing that keeps me committed to socialism, to some degree, today. That is, it does involve democratic planning at all levels.

A number of people claim the same set of ideas, so it becomes a question of choice; and how you end up in one or another organization depends on the extent of your commitment to democratic socialism.

I think the Socialist Party is the socialist group in this country that is committed to democracy, to democratic planning in all aspects of our lives. But this is *not* true of the communists and not as true of various groups moving from the communists over to the Socialist Party—you know, the Trotskyite group, and so on.

Gabriel Almond, in his study of several communist parties in Western countries, reports that the American respondents in his study tended to describe their leaders as "hard, ruthless, cold, remote, and cynical." [8] These attitudes are echoed in comments about American communists made by our respondents:

Actually, when I got out of college, I thought of myself more as a communist than as a socialist. But as soon as I met communists, I knew I wasn't.

It didn't take me a month to find out. Perhaps I couldn't have pinned down at the time why I gravitated to the socialists. But the communists—they were a machine kind of people.

. . .

One didn't like the slavish obedience to Moscow, and the vilification of people who disagreed with them.

. . .

I suppose in a practical way the communists made a socialist out of me because I had some sort of congenital dislike of communist patterns of thinking, and I became a socialist almost to indicate how far I

[8] Gabriel Almond, *The Appeals of Communism* (Princeton, New Jersey: Princeton University Press, 1954).

was from that sort of very dogmatic approach to socialism. I identified myself as a socialist to distinguish myself from the kind of totalitarian approach that the communists had.

. . .

In the socialist movement there was a general spirit of comradeship and friendship and alliance to destroy the capitalist world in favor of a world that was for people and not for profit.

This meant that there was a basic unity there. And this has always characterized the socialist movement. And it has been destroyed everywhere by the communists—everywhere they moved in—because they consider people as things, as tools to use.

This particular issue is still very much alive for the older members of the Socialist Party. A great deal of residual bitterness and anger exists which, perhaps, would not be as strong had their competitors, the communists, not been in a movement which also traced its intellectual origins to Marx. It is easier to forgive people with whom one has nothing at all in common. There is, however, very little of the "I told you so" attitude among the leaders when they refer to the disillusionments of the American Communist Party with the Soviet Union, particularly as a result of the purges of the mid-1930s in the Soviet Union and of Khrushchev's revelations after Stalin's death regarding the injustices of the Stalin regime. The tone of our respondents' remarks on this subject is one of hollow victory rather than vindication.

INTELLECTUALISM

In discussing the reasons for joining the Socialist Party, the exposure to socialist theory and socialist ideas through reading is the one which is given most frequently by the leaders. While several reasons are usually given, this is mentioned by more leaders than other factors such as economic deprivation, peer influences, family influences, etc.

All of our respondents regard themselves as intellectuals. Regardless of social origins, the concern with ideas, meanings, history, and facts is a predominant orientation of our respondents and is strikingly evident in the content of the interviews.

Often, particularly for leaders who started out as laborers, membership in the Party is regarded as having provided a strong impetus to incipient intellectual interests and a channeling of the desire to accumulate knowledge and to apply this knowledge to the conduct of their lives:

In March, 1890, a union was formed in my industry, the ladies garment industry. I joined the union that same month, and I became active in the socialist movement. I participated in the first May Day demonstration in this country in 1890.

At that time, I knew very little about socialism. I had read a few small five-cent pamphlets in Yiddish which were a popularization of socialist principles. I couldn't get very much out of them, but there was enough to interest me.

In the socialist movement we heard for the first time that we were regarded as human beings with human rights. That was the attraction for us, and that's why I entered it. My interest in studying it intellectually came later.

I might say that it was because I entered the movement that I became interested in learning German—so that I could read socialist literature in the German language more effectively. I never spoke German, never knew German. Even after I taught myself to read it, I never used German in that way. But I read a great deal.

I have all of Marx in the original; Kautsky; Lasalle. At first the Gothic script in which the German was printed cut into my eyes. But I managed to overcome that. After the first War, that type of German script was dropped. They then used the Latin script which made it much easier for me.

In the early days of the Socialist Party, the intellectuals within the leadership of the Party served as models for many working class rank and filers in the East:

Joining the Party was almost a natural where I lived and where I worked. I think the Socialist Literary Society gets the major credit for young people joining the Socialist Party and the movement at that time.

They were a group of young people—college boys. At first they wouldn't admit any women members; it was just a young men's organization. So, we decided to petition the Executive Board of the Society to admit women.

They spent time debating the pros and cons, and then finally decided it really wouldn't hurt if they did admit women. So, we were admitted to membership in the same basis as the men.

And they never regretted it because I don't have to tell you that the club room we occupied on East Broadway changed its appearance with our coming there. I recall cleaning and embroidering and decorating, and it really looked nice.

Well, this organization, I think, was responsible for getting the younger people, through the classes and lectures, into the socialist movement. Anyone prominent in the movement who would come to New York, like Jack London, would come to the Socialist Literary Society before going anywhere else. Vandervelde came from Belgium. And all the visitors were eminent men—writers, lecturers, politicians.

That was really what started us in the movement and from there you graduated, when you were old enough, and you joined the Socialist Party. And then you belonged to a certain district. I belonged to the 8th Assembly District.

And there you had men like Morris Hillquit and Meyer London, who came and talked to us on socialism, on politics, on elections.

Now, they were very excellent speakers; both London and Hillquit, and Jack Pankin and Jack Garrity and a lot of others. They addressed the people in simple terms. And they didn't have to go far afield to get the people to listen to their description of factory conditions. We knew it perhaps better than they did! But they could express themselves, and we couldn't.

You begin to read the labor papers. Then you feel that you must somehow get a better understanding of what it is all about. You see around you the poverty and misery, and you know from your own experience about the conditions under which you live and work.

And if you have any brains at all, it doesn't take long for you to realize that this is the place where you belong—that the Party offers some help, some change. And you want to have a part in making the change.

You become active. You learn how to speak in public, and you learn how to lead, more or less, and you learn to value people who know more than you do.

I couldn't go to any public school because of the conflict in hours. We worked overtime and it was a matter of keeping your job or going to school. So, you kept your job—you had to.

But it was true then, and I think it is true today, that if you really want to learn, you can learn without going to school. School helps, of course, but there has to be the will and desire to know.

I think the Socialist Literary Society was a tremendous help to the young people of the East Side in those days. And some of the members have emerged to be great people—Adolf Held, for example, who was one of the college boys at the time I joined.

And there were a number of other people who were part of that movement, which was a combination of the intellectuals and the people who worked in the shops, you see.

There were the college boys, and there the girls who worked for a living and who came to the meetings in the evenings after supper.

Intellectual discussion and argument were, and are, an important aspect of membership in the Party and of the self-definition as a socialist:

One of the great virtues of the socialist movement was that it spurred you to read a lot. It was sort of a game you know. Young deer go around butting their heads against each other in the process of growing up. And young radicals do the same thing, except they do it by throwing citations at each other.

And if you were quick with a good citation, you got satisfaction and prestige. That was always the great chip in the game.

In the early 1930s, discussions still contained the vision of victory:

In time, what was initially a concept, a vague concept, of building a better world, became for me a highly intellectual approach as to what socialism was—the road to power, strategy, methodology.

And we were all junior strategists, planning the revolution. We would have long discussions on the road to power. And if any of the old publications were found, we would have amateurish debates on the particular subject for hours.

I can assure you of this: I think at that time, as I look back—in retrospect—I was probably more secure in my point of view about knowing what to do and how to do it than I am at the moment. I was very certain of everything.

The loss of certainty is a persistent motif in the interviews, particularly with the younger generations, as we shall see when we examine the leaders' beliefs about the future of socialism.

For many of the leaders, membership in the Party was a bridge not only to wider political horizons, but to wider intellectual horizons of a nonpolitical nature:

> I don't know if I had a Russian soul and I was terribly lonely and membership in the Party filled the spot. But I'm sure that it must have filled something. Because what it did do is fill a tremendous amount of time in my life. . . .
>
> There were lots of activities. There were discussions. There were meetings. There were outdoor meetings. There were rallies. There were picket lines. . . .
>
> There was activity, companionship, and intellectual excitement. And by the way, the intellectual excitement carried over not only into readings about socialism and strategy to accomplish socialism, but other readings, other books. I was introduced to an intellectual world alongside of it. And it was very exciting.

Earlier in this chapter I noted that certain characteristics which our respondents attribute to themselves or to other leaders of the Socialist Party are believed to be at least partly responsible for the political failures of the Party. This is true of the idealism of the Party leadership and its highly ethical stance with regard to politics.

The intellectualism of the Party leadership, particularly as reflected in its preoccupation with issues, is also considered by some leaders to have been detrimental to political success:

> We, as people who were leaders of the Party, should have had more organizational sense. I suppose that this was inevitable with the kind of people we were, the kind of people who were attracted to the socialist movement—intellectuals.
>
> We were so involved with issues that we did not stop to think about the impact that doctrinal struggles could have upon us as an organization.

In all of human affairs, you've got to give priority to survival. The one compromise you must always make is in relation to the issue of survival.

There may be things that *ought* to be done, but if the doing of them is going to destroy you, then you've got to postpone doing them. So I think there was bad organizational judgment.

The relationship between means, ends, and values is not a simple one.

The leaders' qualities of character: the strong sense of ethics, the intellectualism, the sensitivity, and the tolerance, give rise to certain predicaments and dilemmas in the realm of political action. On the one hand, these traits inspire a concern for human needs and an avowal of public responsibility for the welfare of the people; on the other hand, they inhibit the use of force in the struggle against less principled and less humanistic political opponents. The imperatives of power and of ethics are often not easily reconciled.

CHAPTER II

THE DECISION TO JOIN

THE decision to join a social movement is generally a cumulative process involving a number of predisposing factors and a precipitating factor. In their discussions of the background and the events leading to the decision to join the Socialist Party, the leaders always recall various influences.

I mentioned in Chapter I that the influence most frequently cited is the exposure to socialist theory and ideas through reading. Economic deprivation or exploitation, either personally experienced or observed, are mentioned almost as often. Family and peer group influences are stressed somewhat less, and other factors such as exposure to leaders and personal need or psychological reasons are referred to even less frequently.

Economic deprivation is stressed far more by the World War I Generation than by the younger generations. Family influences are more prominent in the Interwar Generation reminiscenses than in the others'. Reading, as an initial impetus, is mentioned by a greater proportion of the World War II Generation leaders. Also, personal need or psychological reasons are given almost exclusively by this generation in their spontaneous recollections of their individual paths into the socialist movement. When questioned directly about the possibility of psychological need as a motivating factor, however, a somewhat different picture emerges, as noted later in this chapter.

READING

In discussing reading as a source of the initial beliefs and insights which were eventually to bring the leaders into the socialist movement and into the Socialist Party, the Marxist classics are not named by any of our respondents. A few leaders, primarily in the World War I Generation, refer to reading these classics but usually after they had joined the Party or as a continuing part of the process of socialization. For those who were not socialized into the movement by their families or peer groups, the initial stimulus was often provided either by novels or popularized social criticism which was read during a period of intense search for meaning, usually in early adolescence. The novels of Upton Sinclair and Jack London seem to have been enormously influential. Usually one favorite book or author, whose effect was particularly moving, started the process of active or deliberate political self-identification:

It started really because I grew up obviously during the depression and came to an age when one started thinking, started reading about things.

As I recall, I started doing a fair amount of reading in things like Stuart Chase's books. *Rich Land and Poor Land* is one that comes to mind. It is a rather magnificent thing on conservation and so on.

And I began to think about things. I must have been about fourteen. I was born in 1925, so this would be about 1939 or 1940. . . .

I remember in the fall of 1940 during the presidential campaign, we used to have arguments, the kids around the lunch table, at school. A lot of my friends, kids in class, were Democrats. And there were a few Republicans. Then—I'm kind of argumentative anyway—when the argument was going strongly Democrat, I would attack the Democrats. And then when it went strongly Republican, I'd attack the Republicans.

Finally, I remember very clearly a friend of mine turning and saying, "I've been listening to you, and who the hell *are* you for?" The only name I could think of was Norman Thomas. So I said, "Norman Thomas." Then I decided I'd better find out what I was for, really.

About the same time I caught a radio program by Norman. He used to throw in a line at the end of every radio program saying, "Write in" and so forth. I remember being tremendously impressed because all he would get was fifteen minutes on the radio, and in that fifteen minutes, he seemed to get more said than either of the other candidates got into a whole hour.

So I wrote in. And I remember I got a package with the *Socialist Call* and some other literature. The Party that year put out a pamphlet called *Tweedledee and Tweedledum* which seemed to fit my thinking.

And I began to read. I began to read whatever books on socialism I could get from the library—some of Thomas' books and more things like Stuart Chase and a little bit of Marx, the standard kind of things, the *Communist Manifesto* and so on.

I became, by conviction, a socialist, although there were no socialists in the town where I was born and grew up. In fact there were no socialists at all in that part of the state in 1940.

My contact with the socialist movement was really only through the *Socialist Call* and books until after the war. I went into the Army in '43 and got out in 1946, on January 5th. I had come home on leave, actually, because I remember going down to Boston, and I was still in uniform.

I walked into the Socialist Party office in Boston. A little fellow with big glasses that made him look like an owl was there. I came in with my uniform on, and he looked up with a great deal of surprise. I said, "I want to join the Socialist Party." He said, "You do?" He handed me a card, and I signed up.

Reading can be a precipitating factor, where other factors such as family and neighborhood influences have played a predisposing role, and where there *are* socialists in town:

I came to it easily. My parents had come to the United States in 1905 and had been socialists even before coming here. They were not politically active people. They belonged to an emigré political group in a vague sort of way—the Russian left social revolutionary elements here.

They were connected occupationally with Jewish socialist institutions. My father worked as a proofreader for the *Jewish Daily Forward*° and other papers, most of which had a socialist orientation. My mother worked as a writer and lecturer for the Workmen's Circle.°°

° A Yiddish language newspaper which had a socialist viewpoint until the mid-1930s.
°° A Jewish fraternal order with a socialist orientation.

But I must say that while socialism as a general orientation was in the home, there was no effort on their part, and I think really no anticipation on their part that I would get interested in the Socialist Party. . . .

I joined when I was not quite thirteen—in 1928. It was right before Easter vacation. Isn't it funny, these memories have been buried for at least twenty years. Or thirty, I don't know. In a history class, when papers were assigned, I said I wanted to do a paper on the Socialist Party. I remember that I was not a good student; certainly not a serious student.

I remember going to the Rand School* library day after day during that vacation, and just reading everything in my own manner which is: only original materials, not someone else's history. I remember reading the old Party papers; they had all the old files on the shelves. And I came away feeling that I knew all about the Socialist Party, and that this is where I belonged.

I joined the Party on the week of my thirteenth birthday so I can't forget it. It was right here at 181st Street and Broadway. There was a very big flourishing Socialist Party branch here in Washington Heights.

I remember coming and sitting on the steps waiting for the meeting that had been announced in the weekly Party organ which was the *New Leader*. It was quite a different *New Leader* from what it has become in these latter years; it was really just a Party hack organ in those days.

And I came and sat and waited. An hour after the announced meeting time, someone came and unlocked the headquarters, and people started to drift in. And I said that I wanted to be a member.

Then we went right into the mayoralty campaign, and I guess almost from the first night this became my activity. I was there, I guess, five nights a week. . . . It became the whole focus of my life, and I must say it's remained that, basically, even though I left the Socialist Party a great many years ago.

The love of reading is mentioned by many respondents in their recollections of their search for political identity. For these leaders, reading was an integral part of the multifaceted process of becoming a socialist:

* A school supported and operated by the Socialist Party until the mid-1930s.

I joined the Young People's Socialist League in the late summer of 1932, at which time I was thirteen years old. In a general way, I'd been influenced by my family I suppose, insofar as my mother had been a member of the ILGWU* and a devoted socialist.

My father had died when I was six months old so I had no recollection of him, but my mother had been an active union person.

Partly, I suppose, because of the milieu in which I arose, moving toward the Socialist Party was sort of a natural development. As a kid, I used to go around and listen on street corners. The SP was still quite active on the lower East Side. It didn't have much of a party at that time, but during the depression, they began to expand considerably, and there was a lot of public speaking at that time.

I suppose the one book which gave me a kind of emotional relationship to the Party, more than any other, was Upton Sinclair's *The Jungle*, which I read just about the time I decided to join the Party. It moved me very deeply. . . .

I'd always been a great reader, partly because of the circumstances of my upbringing. My mother was away working in a factory shop, and I was alone most of the day after school.

And when I was a kid I used to read a lot of those paperbacks—I don't mean paperbacks—those little cheap novels. I read two or three a day. I think I read every Gary Grayson, Baseball Joe, Bomba the Jungle Boy, The Allies, Nick Carter, Frank Merriwell, Dick Merriwell, Leggo Lamb—you name it.

You'd buy them and then you'd trade them so you only needed three or four, and then you simply traded your way through, and you read them all. I used to read a lot. I suppose one of the things it tends to do is you get quick comprehension and a fairly good memory. These always stood me in good stead.

This carried over. The habit of reading carried over in terms of reading a lot of history, economics, things of that sort. I remember the first book I tried to read after Upton Sinclair's *The Jungle* was John Stuart Mills' *Principles of Political Economy*. I was thirteen at the time. I don't know why I read it.

There used to be a wonderful library branch on Second Avenue and Lime Street close to where I lived. And they had open shelves. I remember that 300 or so was theology, and 330 was economics in the old Dewey Decimal System that we used to have.

* International Ladies Garment Workers Union

I wandered into economics, and the first thing I saw was John Stuart Mills' *Principles of Political Economy*—two nice fat volumes, and a chapter on socialism at the very end.

I took those out and started reading them. I don't remember if I really understood them at the time. I thought I did; I probably didn't. But the intellectual element, you know, was very important. . . .

And at the same time, there was a very clear awareness of the kind of world I was living in. I suppose to be growing up at a time when we were very poor, aware of the fact that something was wrong with the entire system, again, made a tendency toward socialism quite natural.

The first eight or nine years of our lives—I had an older brother—my mother worked in a shop, and she was subject, of course, to the vicissitudes of slack and small pay in the industry.

And we never lived in an apartment with a toilet in the house. We lived in those old backyard tenements, so-called "Old Law Tenements," and in early years we used to have a toilet down in the yard. We had to go down at night in the yard. In later years, we had a toilet in the hall.

So the sense of slum housing, the sense of poverty was, you know, very much in my mind. And the combination, I think, of the Upton Sinclair novel, plus the Norman Thomas campaign, which was going on at that time, and the influence of a friend who was a member, led me to join the YPSLs at that time.

The actual decision to join always involved a combination of causal factors, some seemingly fortuitous, some deliberate and conscious.

ECONOMIC DEPRIVATION

The oldest generation, some of whom had been manual laborers before assuming a position of leadership in the Party, stress economic deprivation and exploitation, personally experienced or observed, as primary factors in their decision to become socialists:

My immediate interest in the socialist movement and what I supposed it represented, was relief from the sweat shop. Like all others, I suffered very bitterly in the sweat shop. My father was a sweat shop worker also. The earnings were very small; the work week was without a beginning and without an end. There was no regulated work week; one worked as many hours as one could physically stand: 15, 16, 17, 18, a day—just as much as you could stand.

There were two categories of employers: the manufacturers were those who cut the garments, and the contractors were those to whom the garments were sent to be sewn. It was a very complicated situation. The manufacturers were almost exclusively German Jews. They came to this country at least a generation ahead of us, and there was a deep chasm between us.

It was not only the economic one—the employers and workers—but also what you might call a nationalist one. They called us, in their own language, "Ostjuden"—Eastern Jews, who came from the Russian ghetto.

They had nothing but contempt for us. They didn't like our language; they didn't like our way of life; there was no common contact between us and them. And also it was because they had come here so long before and had succeeded in establishing themselves while we were still in the sweat shop.

They organized the Jewish public charities. It is a common practice for Jews whenever they come to a new place to form their charity organizations so that their people may not become a burden to the general population. In that spirit, which was very good, they established the Jewish charities.

They had their headquarters on 8th Street, and to us, the Ostjuden, this was known as the 8th Street. It was organized exclusively for us, the Ostjuden. And the treatment was accordingly. It was not only by the people who hand down charity to people who depend on it, but by people who were *able* to hand it down—they belonging to a superior race and we belonging to an inferior race.

So, all around, my people, including myself, were so situated as to look forward always, and steadily, to something that would give us relief. The socialist movement brought that.

Sometimes the decision to join involved a conception of the Party and its functions which reflected particular group ties or goals. An example of this is the tendency for respondents from the labor movement to define Party goals and functioning in terms of labor's goals, in their retrospective accounts of the Party and the movement. Another example is the definition of Party goals by a Jewish World War I Generation respondent whose major reason for joining was to alleviate economic suffering, but who was motivated by additional goals deriving from group loyalties:

I was born on the other side, and I came here as a youth of twelve years of age. And like all the youngsters and all those people who came here from Russia, we had been hounded and exploited by the czarist government.

We were fresh from the pogroms and all kinds of impositions, and when we came to this country, we rebelled against all the things we had left in the old country.

Here, we saw a chance to open our mouths and our eyes, And, of course, the first thing we did was to join some kind of movement. The socialist movement was the one to join. We didn't know of any other movement that would strive toward the liberation of our people from the yoke of czarism and all kinds of other oppressions.

The goal was freedom above all else. Largely the movement then— this was 1907—was directed and carried on especially here in New York by foreigners who were in opposition to the regime in Russia.

It's true that at that time the movement had quite a goodly number of native Americans, liberals who attempted to lead the movement. But for us, the main current, the main driving force was the desire to fight for the liberation of the people that we left behind.

We hoped in the first place by being free ourselves here, to influence somewhat, and in someway, and somehow, the feelings of the American people as a whole to free our people on the other side. . . .

After a while, we became really active on the American scene and devoted more and more time to the American situation.

After a while, with acculturation and new reference groups, goals were redefined.

The leaders who are of middle-class origin were usually brought into contact with poverty and the economic sufferings of the poor through their occupational or educational activities. This gave impetus to the process which was later to culminate in the decision to join the Party:

I guess my interest dates from 1918–1919 when I came East to go to college. I hadn't had any real contact with socialism that amounted to anything before those days, although the movement was in my consciousness because even in the Middle West, Debs was known and the Debsian type of socialism was known.

I remember I had an old uncle who had heard Debs once, and that had converted him for life. And he used to talk about it, but I wasn't interested in politics at that time. I was just a kid. In Michigan, this was.

But when I came East from the West Coast and saw some of the poverty and saw how some people lived, particularly in New York, I was rather shocked by something I had never seen before—all that poverty. And so I became interested in the movement.

I guess Upton Sinclair had quite an influence on me, because I read many of his books and became quite interested in the movement through that.

But I didn't become a socialist or a member of the Party; I just had an interest in it. Later I began to get associated with people who thought in political and radical terms. And, then, I decided to join.

The process of joining a social movement, as we see again, is always a cumulative one.

FAMILY

In social movements which continue for two or more generations, membership in the movement can be transmitted from parent to child by the same process as membership in a church or any other established voluntary association can be transmitted. The appropriate norms, attitudes, and values are internalized by the child through identification with the parent, a process which is usually not deliberate or conscious. Since children live in relatively circumscribed communities, they may not be exposed to competing norms and values until adolescence or adulthood.

Early indoctrination is particularly effective because of the extreme dependence of the young child upon his family. The child emulates the models that are most available to him. Schools and neighborhoods, insofar as they tend to contain people who are relatively homogeneous in terms of class, may provide other models who confirm and reinforce the attitudes and values appropriate to a particular kind of political behavior.

The relative monopoly of sources of information which parents exert during the early childhood years may predispose the child to membership in particular types of social movements. If the child, as he grows older, encounters individuals or political organizations that expound similar values and norms, and he is not prone to rebel against the political beliefs of his parents, particularly his father, the joining of a political movement can be simply an extension or continuation into adolescence or adulthood of the process of political socialization.

A vivid illustration of the process of political socialization as revealed in children's play, involving role-playing, appears in an article in the *Daily Worker*, June 11, 1947.[1]

If our Party-building drive can use a mascot, I hereby nominate the four-year-old daughter of the Hy Wallachs. This incredible daughter of the veteran section organizer is a Quiz Kid with a social conscience, the vanguard of the infant masses.

Vicki has invented a game called "Section" which all the kids on the block play. The game starts with "lections" to the Section "exec" (Vicki's always chairman) and lesser committees. Dire is the threat of being removed from the "exec" for scratching a playmate or other unsociable conduct. They have assignments of leaflet distribution (any scraps of paper will do,) and Sunday mobilizations. The grown-ups are somewhat bewildered by some of Vicki's terms. A neighbor recently called on Mrs. Wallach to find out what Vicki had in mind when she called her daughter "undisciplined."

While "Section" is a game of fascinating words and forms, it is not entirely without content. After a brief Section meeting, the kids dispersed to their homes to urge a boycott of the anti-Negro film, "Song of the South."

Family attitudes and values had little direct effect on the political socialization of the Protestant leaders in our study. At most, the ethics of the parents are considered to be consistent with the choice that was later made:

[1] Cited in David A. Shannon, *The Decline of American Communism* (New York: Harcourt, Brace and Co., 1959), p. 108.

I don't think my mother ever fully approved of my becoming a socialist. My father was dead by that time. I'm quite sure she didn't. But,
nevertheless, her and my family's standard of morality, while open to
criticism from my present point of view, was genuinely from a good
many angles and, in the best sense, Christian, and interested and
concerned. And that was the background.

Since the overwhelming majority of the Protestant leaders
come from middle-class backgrounds, their becoming socialists
seems more tied to intellectual persuasion than to economic interest or political socialization within the family.

In contrast, the Jewish leaders' decision to become socialists,
particularly in the Interwar Generation, was often a culmination
of socializing influences that began within the family in early
childhood:

I entered the movement on July 28th, 1911, the day I was born. My
parents were both socialists, and I learned to read at the age of four on
the *New York Call*.

When we were small children, the way to get my younger sister to
do something was to tell her she wouldn't be a good socialist if she
didn't.

My father had joined the Socialist Party in 1905, when he was in
his early twenties. His father had not been a socialist, but he had been
involved in the Revolution of 1848 in Germany and had to skip the
country after that.

My mother's father had been a socialist brewery worker.

The Jewish respondents who were born in Europe brought
their socialist ideology from Europe or were exposed to it in their
immigrant subcultures upon arrival. The second-generation
American Jews, particularly the Interwar Generation, received
the ideology by a process of cultural transmission. Comments
such as, "It was in the air," or "It was a natural where I lived," or
"Everyone was always talking about socialism" are typical. The
parents often acted as mediators in this process of transmission.
They were members of the Party; they had been members of the
Party; they were socialists ideologically; or they were sympathetic
to socialism:

My parents, particularly my father, were socialistically inclined. Neither of them was in the socialist movement—for that matter, they never joined any movement. My father had been a supporter of the Jewish Labor Bund which was the socialist organization in Poland. But after he came to this country, he didn't join any organization except the Journeymen's Tailor Union of which he was once, for a brief time, an organizer.

So, the family and their friends, and my father's associates and fellow workers were socialist, in one sense or another, to one degree or another. And so I was more or less favorably inclined toward the idea of socialism, even as a young man.

After I joined in 1920 I went to Chicago to the national office and began to work there. And I'm glad to remember that my parents didn't stand in the way of my joining even after I announced that I was going on this adventurous trip—away from the family—a thousand miles away.

A thousand miles was a good distance in those days. But, although my parents regretted to see me go, they didn't offer the slightest objection to it—not then, and not subsequently.

. . .

My parents were quite happy about my joining the Party, really. They tended to tag along behind. After I became active, they joined the Party also, and they were loyal members and quite active, and so on.

In contrast, parental tolerance, but not encouragement, was the experience of the Protestant respondents:

When I first came to New York, I was shocked to hear my friends discussing their socialist activities openly in front of their parents. . . .

My parents weren't idealistic people, but I think they were decent people. They were a little unhappy about my being a socialist, but they never really interfered with any of our opinions.

They were unhappy about a lot of other things that happened, but they never interfered with our right to read whatever we read or to think whatever we thought.

For many of the second-generation American respondents, becoming a socialist was part of the normal process of growing up in the family and in the neighborhood in which they lived:

Why did I join? Well, my family was socialist. I guess that's probably it. We lived on Hart Street, which was a rather socialist neighborhood. The background was kind of socialist.

As far as I was concerned, the Democrats and the Republicans were
about the same thing. I didn't know the difference. I didn't see any
difference.

And there were problems. At that time, Stuart Chase's *Tragedy of
Waste* was around, and there was plenty of reason to be against the
system. So, at least in my own mind, the thing to do was to join a
movement of protest. And the movement of protest was the Young
People's Socialist League.

And I suppose in our own minds we had constant debates as to
whether we ought to be in the Young Socialist League or the Young
Communist League or the Young Anarchists.

It was not unusual for us to have these constant, running arguments
on the *-isms*. I suppose that was a major activity. There wasn't too
much debate on whether you should be with one of the *-isms*. That
was a normal thing.

We liked to think of ourselves as having been radicals who were
challenging our society, but I am not sure that's right because we had
been brought up in an environment where to be a radical was basically
to be a conformist.

You were kind of aware of the fact that most of the world didn't
agree with you, but that didn't make any difference. In the circles
in which you were likely to move, the people with whom you were
likely to talk—pretty homogeneous people—we were really just going
along, in a sense.

And the Young People's Socialist League had a very active life. You
had meetings which gave you a chance for activity. You made
speeches. There were a lot of social activities—hikes and so on. It was
a lot of fun. And the socialist movement met all of those needs.

In retrospect, it takes on a different meaning I suppose. I think the
reasons we actually had in our heads were valid reasons: that the
society was sort of at dead center. It wasn't moving very much. There
weren't movements around.

I discovered later on that there were many people who were writing,
"This is the lost generation." Well, not my generation. The grown-up
generation, the postwar generation of 1920, was the age of the flapper

and a period of minimal ideas, push, and social strife and movement.

Theoretically, it also was the era of prosperity, except that I never saw it. Nobody ever had to convince me about the fact that this was not an affluent society. It wasn't affluent, period. That was it. My father was always in and out of jobs, and in and out of money; he never really had money. It never hit total poverty, but it was a low level of existence and that was true of the whole neighborhood.

So I think the reasons we had were probably valid reasons, in and of themselves. In retrospect, of course, there were many other reasons. Basically, these were immigrant neighborhoods. They had not been assimilated by the total society. We were kind of outsiders. So it was not difficult to challenge the whole civilization.

And then the socialist tradition in these areas of Brooklyn, and in many areas of Manhattan, was a very, very real thing. You were raised in it, and you had the impression that the Socialist Party was the majority party in America, if you just depended on your own neighborhood. And it was. In Williamsburg, we elected a socialist assemblyman when I was a kid.

So the movement itself was not an odd and unusual and strange thing. It was kind of a natural thing to be a socialist. You might be a Democrat or a Republican in some other part of the country. In Williamsburg, you could be a Democrat or a socialist. What else could you be? And the Democratic Party was the Party of opposition.

I am sure there were many other motivations if we looked deeply enough into it, but anyhow those were the reason for joining.

I came into the YPSL and became a socialist and have pretty much stayed a socialist.

The World War II Generation, particularly the youngest members, grew up in a different environment. The socialist subculture had a much more attenuated effect on those who are second-generation American Jews and who were born in New York:

When I was seventeen—this was in 1951—I started reading Orwell. It was by accident—an assignment in school—not *1984*, not *Animal Farm*, but the political essays. One of them particularly, "Why I Write," was tremendously influential for me. In it he says, "All my life every word I've written, I've written from the point of view of advancing socialism as I understand it."

And I sort of got the idea that I was a socialist, more and more, but I didn't get involved in an organization, since I didn't know any other socialists.

My father is a photoengraver. He used to work for the *New York Sun,* and then that closed and he went to work for the *Times.* He's a Republican.

Nobody in my family had any kind of political background whatsoever. I'm not a Yiddishist. I wasn't raised in the old social democratic movement in the United States which was largely a Jewish group who were often raised within the framework of a socialist tradition of some sort—The Workmen's Circle—the second-generation ILG functionary type. Lots of them were raised in a family tradition of socialism.

Well, I wasn't. I found out many years later that a second cousin of my mother's in Philadelphia had once been on the staff of the *New Masses.* But I never knew about it and never heard about him. It was not a radical family background at all.

Neighborhood influences are not emphasized by the youngest generation. Only one leader feels that his socialist family background may have had some bearing on his decision to become a socialist, but he does not feel that it was a major factor. Reading and college peer group influences are given greater weight.

As noted later in this chapter, the search for a socialist group and for identity, adolescent rebellion, and other indices of the loss of community appear in the reminiscences of this generation primarily. The search took longer and the decision to join took longer. The decision was not made spontaneously at the age of thirteen or fourteen, but later—during or after college usually.

The Jewish respondents in the World War II Generation, who came to maturity in the 1950s, refer to political differences with their parents:

My background was pretty bourgeois, I guess. My father had a dress factory. Economically, I guess we would be working class, but because he had a factory—I don't know how you would characterize it.

My father was sort of conservative. He really didn't think much about politics, but I think he supported Eisenhower. I never had any political education at all. My father had to be at a very low point to even think about politics. I mean, he wasn't an intellectual. He had very little formal schooling. He was born in Poland.

I think when I was supporting Stevenson, he was supporting Eisenhower. Why, I could never understand, because I don't think that reflected his class interests much. But that's what he did. . . .

And I don't think I came to socialism so much from reading, as I've read very little about it. I think it was mostly activity with people who were democratic socialists, particularly at college where they were most active in the civil rights movement. They seemed to have an intelligent point of view. At the time I was a Stevensonian liberal. This was around '54 or '55.

I was dissatisfied, particularly with the compromises on Civil Rights that the liberals were making at the time and that the Democratic Party was making. . . .

Brooklyn College was really sort of an authoritarian state at that time. It was governed by clubs—fraternities, and social groups. There were no political discussions.

I started to work with some socialist students on the issue of student government and on civil rights, and then we developed personal relations. I became interested in socialism. I went to some of the forums of the ISL* and a lot of the things that they said made sense to me.

I was critical of communism, and they had a conservative attitude toward it. It was a radical democratic criticism of communism and of conservativism in the United States.

They had what is called a "third camp" position on foreign policy which is critical of both sides of the cold war. With the United States supporting France and other dictators that was a reasonable point of view, and I slowly began accepting it.

It was mostly that they were active. They were raising the question of civil liberties and all kinds of questions that, except for the communist and pro-communist groups, the liberals were all very quiet about.

The McCarthy era wasn't really over yet. People were still frightened. And liberalism didn't play such a healthy role in that kind of situation. These people I knew were more outspoken, a little more honest about political things.

* International Socialist League, a Trotskyist youth organization.

But I didn't join the ISL. I joined when it merged with the Socialist Party in 1958.

The experience of the older members of the World War II Generation fuses, in some respects, with that of the Interwar Generation, but family influence is considered minimal:

My parents were active in the Russian socialist Bund, but when they got to the United States, much of it had sort of specifically drifted away, and it didn't come up very frequently.

I think I found my way into socialism largely through two avenues. One was reading. George Bernard Shaw was a very specific influence —his books about socialism, his plays, the prologues to his plays.

I would say I was on a Shaw kick in high school, and the first writing that I did, that I recall now, was some sort of analysis of Shavian socialism in a high-school paper.

My parents were generally sympathetic but there wasn't any specific indication in what they did or said that steered me toward socialism. As an intellectual, I got to it by myself.

And as an emotional environmental force, I got it from the depression—the fact that people were talking and talking about socialism, and one became part of the socialist movement, especially in the areas in which I lived, in New York.

In college, I was part of the generalized non-communist left group which included the YPSLs, so that my friends came from among the YPSLs and we always collaborated. City College, during the depression years, was notoriously favorable to socialist and radical thinking of all sorts, and this sponsored or at least increased my interest in participation.

My interest got deeper subsequently when I got out of college. I became associated with a magazine called *The Modern Quarterly* which was a nondenominational socialist magazine which published articles running the whole range of socialist gamuts from the Trotskyists to the anarchists to socialists. It was very specifically, in the early days, one of the quite vociferous and very specifically anti-communist publications.

So I became part of an intellectual socialist group. I contributed to the magazine, and I helped get others to contribute to it. And I finally became a member of the Socialist Party in 1944.

In areas with strong socialist traditions, differentiating factors made some individuals more interested in the movement than others. We cannot attempt to answer the question of what these factors were on the basis of the data collected for this study. However, one interesting finding does appear: one-fourth of our respondents mention the loss of a parent during childhood. They mention this in association with the discussion of the decision to become a socialist, although no cause and effect relationship is implied.

William Kornhauser argues that receptivity to mass movements is due "primarily to the strength of social ties and not to the influence of class, or any other social status." [2] This would seem to be an oversimplification if not a distortion of the multicausal nature of the decision to join a social movement. We have seen that many of the leaders whose political beliefs were largely determined by family and neighborhood influences certainly did not appear to lack strong group ties. However, the loss of a parent in childhood may have weakened family ties for some of our respondents to the extent that they were more available for positions of leadership in the movement:

My mother had problems. She was a widow. So there wasn't the kind of intimacy that some parents have with children. You know, "What's this all going to mean to you in your future?"

I don't think there was ever a discussion about it. I did what I did. Frankly, if what I did had been challenged by my mother, I doubt whether it would have made any difference, knowing our relationship.

But she didn't. What I did was all right, you know. At least she thought it was all right. If she had any other point of view, she never expressed it. . . .

You know, only about two or three years after I joined, I became a leader of the Young People's Socialist League. I was on the Central Committee and on the Executive Committee.

And what made this possible? I don't know. Maybe I was available. You know, who's the girl that gets married? Who's the girl that has dates? The girl who's available.

[2] William Kornhauser, *The Politics of Mass Society* (New York: The Free Press, 1959), p. 337.

Similarly, whether you're selected for these things because you show particular ability or—I don't know. Maybe others were more engrossed in their studies or more engrossed in their families and, therefore, didn't get that far in the movement.

PEER GROUP INFLUENCES

Group reinforcement and support are essential to individuals whose beliefs do not conform to those of the majority in their society, and who wish to act upon these beliefs.

Robert H. Cooley viewed mass communications as a positive force in modern society, wiping out the feeling of isolation, extending the sense of community to the entire country, and permitting "like minded people in religion, politics, art, or what not . . . to get together in spirit and encourage one another in their peculiarity." [3]

For our respondents, who were potential leaders of a political organization, getting together in spirit was not enough. Where socialist organizations were present in the local community or environment, friendship with an individual who was a member often provided the final link in the journey into membership in the movement. Where there were no socialist groups readily available, a search for the group began. This can be a painful process involving hesitation and uncertainty:

There was something missing in my life at the time—both intellectually and probably emotionally. In intellectual terms, the town I grew up in was no great center. Most of the kids I grew up with weren't heading for college. Nobody could think of going to college in those years. Actually, by the time '42, '43 rolled around, we all thought we were going into the service.

But there were a lot of unanswered questions. We were all old enough to know that the depression had wrecked some of our families —not mine particularly, but a lot of others. And the war was a puzzling thing. And socialism had some answers for those kinds of things. It filled this kind of intellectual gap.

[3] Robert H. Cooley, *Social Organization* (New York: Charles Scribners and Sons, 1927), p. 92.

But it didn't fill the gap emotionally, really, because I certainly couldn't get out of it the kind of sustenance you get from belonging to a group. I wasn't able to find a group to belong to.

I remember very vividly the *Socialist Call* one day carried an announcement. There was a guy whom I met after the war who then was the state Socialist Party secretary. He was going to come to our town to hold a meeting, and people were invited to come.

I tried screwing up my courage. After all, I was only sixteen or seventeen. I was going to go into town that night and see if I could find that place.

But I just never really got enough courage to go to the meeting. Here I was a kid and why should I show up at this adult affair? So I never did go.

Finding the group can be the culmination of years of searching:

Now you must understand that I really started off in college on my own. The college at that time had people who were mostly from the area—very few outsiders, and it was a sort of vocationally oriented school.

And in my day, I was out of fashion on campus. I really was. This was in 1955, and the world was different. The radical world was different. SNCC didn't exist. The Supreme Court decision had come out, but the era of the demonstrations in the South hadn't occurred yet. The radical movement was about as small as it had ever been. . . .

Today there's a whole milieu, a whole world, that didn't exist in 1955. You might say that my mistake was that I was born six years too soon. Six years later and I might have been part of the New Left.

I was an ex-GI, a little bit older than some of the other students. I was interested in jazz somewhat. I was interested in literature. So I started off. And I'm a social enough fellow and I met people—a lot of nice people, good people.

Then I started to meet really interesting people; people who were like me. On campus everyone was very security conscious because it was the McCarthy era. People were being fired right and left for being communists, for being radicals.

It was a very difficult situation. There were faculty members there who were socialists, a couple of them. And there were some old people around town and a few of the youths who were socialists.

Well, they didn't know what to do with me, those folks in town. Here I was, a socialist. I said I was a socialist. I was eager to do work. I was active, and I loved to talk to people about socialism.

Well, they were absolutely frightened to death of me. Holy God, what is this person doing? My God, he's a nut! He talks too much; he's not security conscious.

After about six months they invited me to some parties first and then to some discussions. They invited me just to parties at first because they were very careful about whom they would invite to meetings. They didn't want to be turned in to the FBI or to have anything like that occur.

So eventually, I became a member of the Young Socialist League. This was about '56 or '57. We had maybe one hundred twenty members coast to coast. That was one hundred twenty members on the books. But really—I mean if you took a good look at the one hundred twenty, a great many of them didn't exist.

Some of them were graduate students—one was a thirty-year-old graduate student who kept his membership for God knows what reason. Other people hadn't paid dues. Probably there were fewer real members than the one hundred twenty. And we had no influence, no connections with anything, and no openings into any kind of real political activity.

But I was a socialist, and this was a socialist organization, and I had finally run across it. If I'd run across the socialist organization five years earlier I would have joined then.

The United States is full of people who, all by themselves, in their little towns in one place or another, have thought of themselves as socialists—for all kinds of reasons. They've read books; they had a high-school history course. Socialism makes sense to them. But they've never run across any kind of socialist movement.

Well, I was one of them, and I was prepared to be active. And then I turned active with a vengeance.

The discovery of the group can be a great comfort to those who feel alone in their beliefs:

It was like the falling down of prison walls about my mind; the amazing discovery, after all those years, that I did not have to carry the whole burden of humanity's future upon my two frail shoulders! There were actually others who understood; who saw what had gradually become clear to me, that the heart and center of the evil lay in leaving the social treasure which nature had created and which every man has to have in order to live, to become the object of a scramble in the market place, a delirium of speculation. The principal fact the socialists had to teach me was that they themselves existed.[4]

Once found, the group provides a new basis for friendship and a consciousness of kind:

As for the friends I had, they were quickly replaced by a new set of friendships in and around the YPSLs. I knew fellows, but they were fellows around the block. They weren't very deep friendships.

I think the relationships that were built in the YPSLs were on a higher level. They were more profound, more intellectual, more concerned with the world rather than the trivial sort of thing that fellows on the street corner are concerned with.

. . .

I remember the feeling that I had when I joined because I was so delighted about it. I remember various speakers who would come through on tours. Younger people would come through, and some of the people were so bright, so attractive to me as people that I would be delighted when I found that they read the same books I had read, I know that, he knows that—there's a certain community there.

A sect tends to regard itself as a body of the "elect" set off, through conflict, from a larger religious group.[5] The parallel between religious sects and radical political organizations is often drawn. The recollection of having felt like a member of the elect in relation to other, nonmembers of the Party, appears in the reminiscences:

There's a form of psychological encapsulation which becomes important to people who live within the movement. What's striking to me as I think about it is how early—because I was thirteen or fourteen at the time—and how quickly all this came to the fore.

[4] Upton Sinclair, *The Autobiography of Upton Sinclair* (New York: Harcourt, Brace and Co., 1962), p. 101.
[5] Lewis Coser, *The Functions of Social Conflict* (Glencoe, Illinois: The Free Press, 1956), p. 91.

Debating about society, etc., became much more real than the abstract notions of overthrowing capitalism, you know.

It's much more real to debate with people in the factional life because somehow they were talking the same language. If you talked to kids outside who didn't really know what was going on, they were simply kids who read the newspapers and somehow were not really aware of the forces of history in this way.

It's one of the remarkable things, the way in which a radical movement can create so quickly an atmosphere of its own which has this form of enclosure.

Through the years, the Socialist Party offered selective exposure to ideas and a selective processing of information from the outside world so that the optimism and idealism of the membership could be maintained:

Life within the YPSLs was very different from the overt public life of simply being ideologically against capitalism, or carrying on activities in terms of street corner meetings, propaganda, and such.

There was a kind of double level of activity in which you sort of got involved beneath the surface in a small world which had a kind of enclosure of its own.

You suddenly felt you were riding the wave. People were writing resolutions on the road to power, as if all it took to win power essentially was to write resolutions, and there was a very heady sense of being able to command the forces of history in these terms.

. . .

And there was an extraordinary impulse to read and to study. In some cases, this becomes self-defeating because you read in effect to document a given conclusion that you have already arrived at, and it has all those theological aspects of searching for evidence to support a preconceived view.

But apart from that the more immediate thing is essentially that membership in the party gave you a framework of history and a framework of ideas that foreshadowed what would be happening, so to speak, when the express route of history moved you forward.

The further removed group definitions and group values are from the surrounding society, and the greater the commitment of group members to these innovative values and ideas, the stronger is the tendency to confine one's contacts to people and ideas that sustain these values and ideas.[6] Aside from the comfort derived from associating with like-minded people, there is the possibility of retaining these beliefs and values in pure and uncontested form.

Active membership in the Socialist Party was an all-enveloping way of life, determining not only political activities, but leisure and intellectual pursuits as well. Not only were friendships confined to Party members but marriages were frequently contracted between Party members. In the Communist Party, marriages between Party members were defined as preferable and were referred to as "progressive marriages." [7]

Georg Simmel has pointed out that intragroup conflict is most intense precisely in groups involving the total life of the individual, where interaction is intense, and which exist in opposition to other groups in the society.[8]

Factionalism was a serious problem for the Socialist Party in its period of greater strength. It is still a problem with regard to the issue of realignment. But it is a factionalism of a much attenuated nature (weariness rather than militance tends to be characteristic of opponents in current factional disputes) reflecting, no doubt, the decline of the effect of the Party on its members' lives.

Renegadism is a serious threat to the tight-knit all-embracing conflict group. Louis Coser attributes this to the fact that conflict with an out-group defines the boundaries of an established group, and renegadism threatens to break down these boundaries.[9] Expressions of resentment toward former members who left the Party are not uncommon in the two older generations. This anger is usually expressed in accusations of opportunism, expedience,

[6] For a discussion of the concept of selective exposure, see, Paul Lazarsfeld, Bernard Berelson, and Hazel Gaudet, eds., *The People's Choice* (New York: Duell, Sloan and Pierce, 1944).

[7] Shannon, *The Decline of American Communism*, p. 107.

[8] Georg Simmel, *Conflict and the Web of Group Affiliations* (Glencoe, Illinois: The Free Press, 1955).

[9] Coser, *The Functions of Social Conflict*, p. 69.

plagiarism, ingratitude to the Party, or unwillingness to admit former membership on the part of people who now occupy important positions in the mainstream of American political life. And yet, expressions of antagonism are often tempered with pride in the accomplishments of these ex-socialists.

The World War II Generation leaders express neither anger nor pride in ex-members of the Party. In fact they do not mention Party renegades at all. This undoubtedly reflects the decreased meaning that Party membership has had for them, although almost all are still members. Maintaining boundaries of the Party as an in-group is no longer a necessity, or even a possibility, when younger members of the Party are now working actively within the Democratic Party.

That socialism as a way of life and as a functional equivalent of religion persists in Eastern European countries, at least for the older population, can be inferred from the fact that gravestones in these countries often are crowned either with the cross or with the red star.

How meaningful the socialist ideology is to the younger generations in these countries and in the Soviet Union is a matter of dispute at present. There is no question, however, that the younger Socialist Party leaders whom I interviewed do not have, and have not had, the experience of total enclosure and apocalyptic visions that the older generations experienced and so vividly recall.

In the process of becoming members of the Socialist Party, the older generations were more likely to have encountered socialist peer groups readily available in their local environments. The World War II Generation leaders were more apt to have engaged in a deliberate search for a socialist organization after the disruption of primary group ties—upon entering college or, in one instance, upon being demobilized from the army:

The war was disruptive, in a sense. We were pulled out into the service, and when we came back, we all busted up and went to various parts of the country.

In the unit I served in there wasn't any kind of cohesiveness that would keep you close together after the war. I kept one or two friends from the service, but it wasn't a large enough group to sustain oneself in terms of having friends.

And the Socialist Party gave you almost a ready-made set of friends when you moved from a home town to a new situation. I think that plays a kind of role. I think it's probably true for a lot of socialists.

Anyway, with my kind of ideological commitment, and getting involved with a whole set of new friends in the Socialist Party, I found a home.

Community lost and community regained seems to have been a characteristic experience of this generation. Modern society is a mobile society: geographically, socially (up and down the class structure) and psychically—psychically because modern man, as opposed to traditional man, can and does identify with individuals and groups who are not in his immediate geographic community.

In fact, Daniel Lerner believes that empathic ability involving distant people and places is the distinguishing characteristic of modern man.[10] Lerner's traditional-minded respondents in the Middle East could not conceive of living anywhere else or of being anyone else. In response to the question, "If you were king . . ." they could only reply, "But I could not be king."

Modern man, with the aid of mass communications and developments in rapid transportation, experiences a broadening of his perspectives. He has many more alternatives with regard to aspirations, expectations, and identifications. And he is apt to experience, thereby, a loss of community—a loss of old meanings, faiths, and identities.

In microcosm, this loss is illustrated quite clearly in the reminiscences of the youngest generation. The decision to join the Party, in most instances, occurred after a complete or partial separation from the geographic community. The leaders in this generation dwell at greater length on the fact of an active and, above all,

10 Daniel Lerner, *The Passing of Traditional Society* (Glencoe, Illinois: The Free Press, 1958), p. 50.

independent search for new meanings, ways of life, and solutions.

The finding that the youngest leaders joined the Party after a separation from community, friends, or family seems to be true of the joining of other contemporary social movements by young people. Studies conducted at the University of California, at Berkeley, indicate that students who become political activists are newcomers to the campus: freshman and transfer upper-level and graduate students. Typically, they do not live at home, and they experience feelings of loneliness, anxiety, and disorientation upon arrival at Berkeley.[11]

EXPOSURE TO LEADERS

Exposure to leaders is a factor which is always mentioned in conjunction with other predisposing causes in discussing the decision to join. Often, at least in the World War I Generation, it was the precipitating factor in the process of becoming a member of the Socialist Party. This influence is mentioned less by the Interwar and the World War II Generations, reflecting, no doubt, the declining strength of the Party through the years and also the increasing difficulty in establishing direct communication between leaders and potential recruits to the Party. The days of soapbox oratory are gone, and the prohibitive cost of gaining access to the mass media, particularly television, has severely limited this aspect of the role of leadership in social movements.

Social movements arise, generally, in periods of crisis, when the prevailing values, beliefs, and institutions in a society do not seem, at least to some members of the society, to fulfill certain important human needs or expectations.

The leaders of social movements promulgate new values and new goals that are, typically, condensed into slogans that symbolize the values of the movement and promote the solidarity of its members.[12]

11 Seymour M. Lipset, ed., *Student Politics* (New York: Basic Books, 1967).

12 For an analysis of the role of slogans in social movements, see, Joseph Bensman and Bernard Rosenberg, eds., *Mass, Class, and Bureaucracy* (Englewood Cliffs, New Jersey: Prentice-Hall, 1963), pp. 351–54.

Social movements represent deliberate and coordinated attempts to bring about social change in a society and are distinguished, therefore, from social trends which occur as the result of the aggregate effect of the discrete and uncoordinated actions of millions of individuals.[13] Urbanization, for example, is an unplanned trend which is the result of the uncoordinated decisions of millions of individuals to move from the country to the city.

Intellectuals are generally in the forefront of new social movements because they reflect on ethical and religious questions and seek to understand the world in meaningful terms.[14]

Recruitment of members into social movements and coordination of their activities require communication between leaders and members and between leaders and potential new recruits. Communication, either direct or indirect, is the essential element in the maintenance and growth of a social movement.

With the technological advances in mass communications and transportation in the twentieth century, the possibility of reaching (as well as of controlling) all members of the society arises for the first time in history. The now widely used concept of mass society refers, at the most formal level, to a populous society in which all members can participate in the political process—for purposes of good or evil, conservation, or change.

In traditional societies, social movements directed at the power and privilege of leading strata in the society were usually confined to sporadic revolts, largely because of the difficulty in reaching and mobilizing isolated elements of the population. In urban, industrial society on the other hand, this type of limitation to the scope of social movements no longer exists.

The essence of totalitarianism is absolute control over all aspects of the lives of the citizenry and the suppression of all organized opposition in the society—whether this opposition is institutionalized in the form of a political party, or whether it is a

[13] See Rudolph Heberle, *Social Movements* (New York: Appleton-Century Crofts, Inc., 1951), p. 64, for a discussion of this distinction.

[14] For a discussion of the role of intellectuals in social movements see, Max Weber, *The Sociology of Religion* (Boston: Beacon Press, 1963), Chapt. 8.

budding social movement. The essence of democracy, or the minimum conditions of its existence, is organized opposition in the society and the permanent insecurity in office of public officials.

While American society tolerates movements of opposition, leaders of these movements experience increasing difficulties in communicating with potential recruits because of the enormous costs of buying media time and space. This is reflected in the frequent protests of our respondents about their inability to contact the larger audiences which must be reached in the era of the participant society.

In the United States, third party movements have always been hampered by the fact that a new party, or a small party, cannot hope to achieve victory at the polls in gubernatorial or presidential campaigns. Voters have been hesitant to waste their votes, particularly when there is a lesser of two evils choice available within the two established parties.

The current situation, involving as it does far larger numbers of geographically dispersed voters who must be reached, largely and primarily through the mass media, poses a grave problem for the effectiveness of the democratic process in the United States. Not only is the very existence of organized movements of opposition threatened but, even more seriously, the availability of real choices in the political process is diminished.

PERSONAL OR PSYCHOLOGICAL FACTORS

Since the beginning of the psychological era in the 1930s, motivation has become a focus of analysis and a central preoccupation not only of psychologists but of other intellectuals in this country.

What motivates any particular human act is an extraordinarily complex combination of factors: conscious and unconscious, historical and current, realistic and unrealistic. Nonetheless, the motivation of political dissenters in our society has been a highly popular subject of inquiry since the 1930s, an intellectual vogue which has only recently begun to decline in favor of at least a dual focus on the dissenter and the society in which he lives.

Karl Marx [15] believed that bourgeois intellectuals, because of their ability to comprehend theoretically the laws of history and social change, would join the proletariat and organize and educate it in preparation for the goal of obtaining political power. For Marx, this was a purely intellectual and rational process.

With the popularization of Freudian theory in this country, the rationality of the motives of political dissenters became suspect. Political dissent came to be viewed as an expression of hatred of authority figures and an excessive drive to power, stemming from emotional deprivation and negative identification with parents in early childhood. Harold Lasswell [16] was a pioneer in this type of analysis, and his work was widely imitated. It has been argued that interpersonal discomfort with dominant authority figures encourages a compensating identification with the underdog that leads to reformist political beliefs.[17] And it has also been argued that there is a tendency for moderately damaged father-son relationships to result in a relatively low level of hope, interest, and capacity to criticize existing political structures on the part of the son.[18] The inconsistency in these two types of arguments is not untypical in the literature.

The confusion and inconsistency that exist in the writings on this subject derive from the difficulty in determining motivation objectively, even with the relatively sophisticated techniques now available to psychologists. And most attempts to investigate the motivation of political dissenters have not been made by psychologists.

A central concept in this type of inquiry is that of "adolescent rebellion." From the psychoanalytic point of view, this refers to the tendency for adolescents to replace parents as an object of

[15] Karl Marx, *The Communist Manifesto, 1848* (New York: Appleton-Century-Crofts, 1955).

[16] Harold Lasswell, *The Psychopathology of Politics* (Chicago: University of Chicago Press, 1930).

[17] Robert Lane, "The Need to be Liked and the Anxious College Liberal," *Annals of the American Academy of Political and Social Science*, Vol. 361 (September, 1965), 71–80.

[18] Robert Lane, "Fathers and Sons: Foundations of Political Beliefs," *American Sociological Review*, 24 (August, 1959), 502–11.

love by individuals outside of the family who are "diametrically opposed in every aspect (personal, social, cultural) to the original ones." [19] This occurs, according to the theory, as a reaction formation to repressed erotic attachments to the parents which become dangerous in adolescence because of the development, during this period, of adult genital sexuality. The new love objects may be political leaders who represent the adolescent's ideals.

Throughout the period of greatest vogue in the psychological examination of the motives of political dissenters, class- or stratification-based analyses of political behavior continued, albeit overshadowed somewhat in terms of dramatic appeal. [20]

At present, there is a resurgence of interest in class and familial attitudes and values as determinants of political beliefs, although the psychological focus persists. Whether or not adolescent rebellion is a psychological fact, the present evidence suggests that the political beliefs and behavior of adolescents are far more likely than not to conform to parental attitudes and values. [21]

The increased emphasis recently on social conditions as a factor in political dissent and on political socialization as a nonpathological process has to do probably with the rise of the civil rights movement and the rediscovery of poverty in this country. These phenomena have provided a more obvious basis for political dissent in a period of prosperity.

Because of the growing complexity of the social structure and increased understanding of the effects of religious, ethnic, occupational, and regional identifications on political behavior, present class-based analyses in this country tend to be more refined than in the past. The Marxist formulation of a one-to-one

[19] Anna Freud, "Adolescence," *The Psychoanalytic Study of the Child* (New York: International Universities Press, 1957), Vol. XIII, 269.

[20] See for example, Paul Lazarsfeld, Bernard Berelson, and Hazel Gaudet, eds., *The People's Choice* (New York: Duell, Sloan and Pearce, 1944); Richard Centers, *The Psychology of Social Class* (New York: Russell and Russel, 1961); also, numerous analyses by Marxist or neo-Marxist writers.

[21] See, Herbert H. Hyman, *Political Socialization* (New York: The Free Press, 1959); also, David T. Westby and Richard G. Braungart, "Class and Politics in the Family Backgrounds of Student Political Activists," *American Sociological Review*, Vol. 31 (October, 1966), 690–92.

relationship between class and economic interest is now elaborated to include the fact of multiple statuses in many groups. Class is a many faceted phenomenon in complex industrial society. Concepts such as status inconsistency and status insecurity are utlilized to account for the fact, for example, that today leftist students in this country come predominantly from the upper-middle class, while those on the political right are more likely to be lower-middle class or working class in origin. The former are often economically privileged members of minority groups, while the latter tend to feel insecure about the new status they occupy, or are trying to achieve, or about their borderline status.

Current views on the psychological motivation of political dissenters and members of other social movements are also more precise. They contain a distinction with regard to the level of membership and the degree and kind of commitment to the movement. A distinction is made between marginal members of social movements and the leadership of these movements. These categories of membership and commitment have been variously labeled: exoteric and esoteric membership; [22] extrinsic and intrinsic believers; [23] Reformer I and Reformer II; [24] and instrumental and belief-centered membership.[25] These distinctions differentiate between individuals who join a movement primarily because of personal needs: security, friends, power, material rewards, status, etc., and individuals who join a movement primarily for intellectual and rational reasons: because they believe it has the answers which they are seeking. The current view is that the latter type of individual is more likely to assume a position of leadership in a social movement and is less likely to defect for personal or psychological reasons.

[22] Gabriel Almond, *The Appeals of Communism* (Princeton, New Jersey: Princeton University Press, 1954).

[23] Gordon W. Allport, ed., *Religion in the Developing Personality* sponsored by Academy of Religion and Mental Health (New York: New York University Press, 1960).

[24] Stuart Chase, *The Proper Study of Mankind*, Rev. Ed. (New York: Harper & Bros., 1956).

[25] Hans Toch, *The Social Psychology of Social Movements* (Indianapolis, Indiana: Bobbs-Merrill Co., 1965).

Actually, of course, it would be impossible to determine the exact ratio of personal need to intellectual persuasion in any particular instance of joining a social movement. Also, human motives have a way of becoming independent of the needs from which they originated. Thus, for example, the cultivation of intellectual pursuits for the purpose of furthering a career may become intrinsically gratifying with time. In a recent study, when asked what they would do with a twenty-six hour day, university professors overwhelmingly chose work or work-related activities.[26] It is unlikely that this finding can be attributed solely to the career-building motive. Gordon Allport conceptualized the idea that motives tend to become independent of the needs and beliefs from which they derive as "the functional autonomy of motives."[27]

The applicability of functional autonomy theory to the motivation of individuals in social movements increases with their degree of dedication and responsibility within the movement. Consequently, the attempt to trace motives to remote origins becomes a fruitless, if not irrelevant, endeavor.

As leaders of the Socialist Party, our respondents, have been deeply committed to the Party, its ideology, and goals. An appraisal of the role of personal or nonrational factors in their decision to become socialists is impossible on the basis of the data gathered. An attempt to do this with Communist Party respondents was made by Gabriel Almond using similar data (tape-recorded depth interviews), plus information gathered from psychoanalysts who had patients who were members of the Communist Party. Almond concludes that the high echelon members of the Communist Party in his sample manifested neurotic needs far less frequently than the lower echelon respondents. He recognizes, however, the limitations of his data: "While coding was conservative, a depth interview is hardly a satisfactory basis for making clinical appraisals."[28]

[26] H. L. Wilensky, *Work, Leisure and Freedom: The Gains and Costs of Abundance* (New York: The Free Press, in press).

[27] Gordon W. Allport, "The Functional Autonomy of Motives," *American Journal of Psychology*, 50 (November, 1937), 141–56.

[28] Almond, *The Appeals of Communism*, p. 259.

Questions which can legitimately be asked of the data are: Do the leaders feel that their decision to become socialists was a purely rational one? In this respect, are there differences between the generations which may reflect the rise of the psychological perspective in the 1930s and the recent shift to an increasingly sociological perspective on the part of intellectuals in this country?

As I pointed out earlier in this chapter, in spontaneously discussing the circumstances and influences which led to the decision to join the Party, our respondents mentioned personal need or psychological reasons much less frequently than factors such as reading, or family and peer group influences. Such reasons as loneliness, the need for identity, the desire to express oneself, or adolescent rebellion, when they are mentioned, come primarily from World War II Generation leaders.

However, when asked directly whether they feel there were psychological or irrational factors in their decision to join the Party or if their confidence in their ideas was undermined by the psychological theories about the motivation of political dissenters, a distinct pattern emerges in the replies of various generations.

The majority of the leaders characterize their decision to become socialists as a purely rational one. This is consistent with the finding reported in this chapter, that exposure to socialist theory and ideas through reading is the reason most frequently mentionec by our respondents when discussing their decision to join the Party. When we examine the replies of the different generations, however, we find certain striking differences between them.

With one exception, all members of the World War I Generation who were questioned on this topic feel that their decision was a purely rational one:

I joined the Socialist Party because I wanted to help improve conditions for workers. I wasn't a rebel. I joined the Socialist Party for the same reasons that I joined many other organizations: to see certain goals carried out.

I didn't feel there was anything different about me. I was idealistic; I wanted to help people. Money wasn't important to me, and the mercenary values of our society didn't affect me that much.

I could have gone much further, much faster, in the Democratic

Party, but I didn't and don't believe attempting to achieve socialist reforms within the established parties can ever work because of the necessity to compromise. And after a while, your goals as well as your means are compromised.

. . .

Was my confidence in my ideas ever shaken by the psychological theories about radicals and what motivates us? Never, not for one moment!

What motivates us is values—standards of decency and social justice and social progress. Nothing less.

Only one leader feels that there were emotional or psychological factors involved, and he is a psychologist. One other leader, while claiming that his own decision was purely rational, believes that other members of the movement may have been motivated by psychological problems:

I was not in revolt against my father. Becoming a socialist for me was an intelligent decision based on existing social conditions. If I hadn't been a rebel, I would have been a moron.

But this was not so of some of the younger people who joined the Party in the thirties or the forties, or of the communists—those people who now violently repudiate their socialist past.

With the one exception, the leaders in this generation, while aware of the psychological theories, do not accept them or do not feel that they apply to themselves. They entered the socialist movement during the period of relatively unregulated capitalism, when the rationality of their decision seemed quite obvious and before depth psychology had provided the tools for questioning their motives. The psychological perspective has not penetrated their thinking. A few leaders in this generation seemed to have difficulty in understanding the questions about the possibility of psychological factors in their decision to join; the two younger generations had no such problem.

In stark contrast to the World War I Generation, only one leader in the Interwar Generation seems to feel that his decision did not involve personal or psychological needs, but, actually, he avoids a direct answer:

Those theories never bothered me because I was pretty clear about what I wanted and what I wanted to do. . . . Oh, I had problems. My mother died when I was twelve and then, later, my father remarried, and I was living with him and my stepmother for a while. And I couldn't get along with her at all. She was very opposed to my socialist activities because the neighbors would talk.

But I thought that was too bad for her. My activities didn't bother me. . . .

I decided that because I was a rebel in terms of my philosophy of economics and political life, I would be particularly careful not to be a rebel in things that didn't matter.

In other words, I had the approach that I wouldn't violate traffic laws; I wouldn't violate any laws except those that I considered I had to on the grounds of conscience, and that I wouldn't be a beatnik in terms of the way I dressed (we didn't use the term "beatnik" but "bohemian") or the way I lived.

I decided I would live as orderly a life as possible, partly because I saw around me a lot of people who came in as flaming revolutionists and burned themselves out very quickly.

All of the other leaders in this generation who talked about this subject, feel that emotional need or psychological factors were involved in their choice. They argue, however, that this does not invalidate their ideas:

It is perfectly correct that if you choose to analyze the individual motivations, the individual factors which led each of us into the socialist movement, you would find subjective psychological explanations for why this one came, coming from a reactionary family, and that one, coming from a home of poverty, and this one, from a home of wealth, and that one, from a home of radicalism.

Each one had his own pattern. But the fact that we came to it by this pattern really had nothing to do, positively or negatively, with the validity of our social analysis.

I've always felt that way, and I've always been able to say, "If we want to analyse why Norman Thomas became a leader of the Socialist Party instead of a leader of the church, we can look deeply enough into his family background, his emotional background, his etc., etc., background, and we can find the answer."

But having found the answer, and having found let us say, that it goes back to X, Y, and Z, the subject closes. It doesn't make him less a great socialist leader—more correct, if he's correct, or more wrong, if he's wrong.

For some of the leaders in this generation, the psychological theories have been troublesome thorns through the years, and much thought and introspection has been spent on the question of their motivation in becoming political dissenters:

I think it's a terrible thing that those psychologists and psychiatrists have done to us because they completely . . . well, not completely, because they haven't succeeded in destroying our confidence. But if they had their way, I think so many of us would come out with the view that we're not really free agents.

If I'm for capitalism, it's because of psychology. If I'm for socialism, it's for the same reasons. Whatever I am, it's not because of me but because of something outside of my control.

I've thought about that. I thought about it a great deal in the 1940s. I'll tell you what was very helpful in resolving it in my thinking. It was one man's story—a parable that I read.

I don't know that Koestler spelled it out in those terms, but this is the way I recall it. Some day I must go back and take a look at it.

You remember Koestler's *Arrival and Departure*. In it he tells a story. He discusses how Euclid arrived at his geometry. Euclid found that his wife was having an affair with somebody else.

He went down to the seashore thinking that he ought to drown himself. He sat there on the seashore debating what he should do. Because he was involved in a triangle, he drew a triangle.

And then, because he had drawn the triangle, he got interested in the angles. And, out of this, came Euclidean geometry.

The meaning of the parable is: we've got Euclidean geometry only because Euclid's wife slept with another man. This is purely psychological. Now, suppose it's true? Does that invalidate all the findings that are involved in Euclidean geometry?

Now maybe it's true that my father looked askance at me and I'm in rebellion against my father, and, therefore, I took a critical look at my society. That doesn't invalidate the conclusions which I came to about society.

The answer as to whether or not capitalism and the greed for profit, and the involvement of human beings in the grubby pursuit of material things—whether or not this is valid, is not determined, really, by what my father did to me.

Maybe I was able to see it because of what my father did to me. But there is still some objective criterion which I can apply to my observation of society.

In comparison with this generation, the World War II Generation is somewhat more apt to feel that theirs was a purely intellectual or rational decision. This may reflect the decline in the supremacy of the psychological focus in recent years:

Those theories were very big in the fifties. I think they went along with the McCarthy period. You know—you shouldn't be a radical. American society was so terrific. There was no poverty. Everyone was living in affluence.

I guess those theories could bother you, particularly if you're an isolated radical. But I think the fact that I was active with people who considered themselves socialists helped.

I mean, you find decent people in the movement, and you don't accept the psychological interpretation of people's motivations—that radicals are different psychologically from other people. I think being in the organization sort of helps people overcome that.

And I think that it's much less of a problem today, because everybody sees what problems there are in society and what real basis there is for radicalism.

I think the civil rights movement really undercut that ideology. There was too much meaningful protest for people to say, "Anybody who protests is a nut." I think it was really the civil rights movement more than anything else that made that kind of approach much less meaningful.

I don't think it's bought by so many people now. The academicians used to buy it and make a living out of it. But I don't think they're doing so good with it now.

In the World War II Generation those who feel that there were personal or irrational factors in their decision to become socialists argue again most frequently that this does not invalidate their ideas:

You'd have to be an idiot not to understand that if one per cent of the American population joins small groups of people, you know, who are distinguished chiefly by the fact that they disagree with everybody else around them, there must be some irrational motivation there. There has to be.

And there's a certain kind of comfort in being in a small, radical sect. As I said before, the best and the worst join the socialist movement. And some aspects of the worst outshadow the best. There's a lot of neurotic interaction. There's a lot of the defensive kind of thing.

But the ideas are greater than the people who express them. They've been expressed by hundreds of thousands of people in all sorts of societies, under all sorts of circumstances.

I may be crazy. I won't disagree with anybody who says I'm crazy. I'm crazy as a bedbug. And we're all crazy in different ways. We're all not that much alike. We're individuals.

Now one of the things that kept us sane—that kept some people sane—is the socialist movement. The socialist movement offered some people who would have gone off the deep edge a certain mechanism, a certain place, a function within the society. It was a help to do something for some people. Other people it may have made sicker. You know, exacerbated certain things.

But I don't believe it's intellectually respectable to dismiss a man's ideas and say, "I'll merely look at your personality." There's something rather disgraceful about that whole technique.

While more members of this generation claim to have been rationally motivated in joining the movement, there is also, on the other hand, a greater awareness of the psychological perspective in this generation and more sophisticated use of psychological theory:

I think it's always helpful to know what the basis of a movement is. I think, for example, the pacifist and the Marxist movements represent personality types.

The Marxist movement is traditionally a masculine movement. It's a rigid and orthodox and logical movement based on logic entirely and, therefore, a very masculine movement. The pacifist movement is a yielding, theological, intuitive movement, and they attract different personality types without any question. . . .

Very gentle people go into the pacifist movement—sometimes. Sometimes you find very, very violent people going into the pacifist movement. They have to sublimate terrible aggressions, terrible hatreds, and, therefore, they become pacifists. . . .

I think the conservative movement, around Buckley, is a movement that attracts people who have very serious personality problems in terms of questioning their own masculinity. They, therefore, deliberately seek out the most violent possible solution, one that will make them feel virile by advocating virile things like bombing children.

This kind of conceptualization of events and human behavior would be inconceivable to almost all members of the World War I Generation and probably to many members of the Interwar Generation.

The concept of identity is referred to only in this generation:

I went to City College where you almost had to define yourself politically on the left simply to have an identity or to distinguish yourself from others.

Adolescent rebellion as a likely or an unquestionable factor in the decision to become a socialist is mentioned by only four leaders. All but one are members of the World War II Generation.

The theory can be invoked when it obviously applies:

What drew me directly to socialism at that time was the 1940 campaign between Roosevelt and Wilkie. I must have been ready to become a socialist. I do remember, very vividly, listening to the Republican convention on the radio that year.

As you remember, it went on all night long with the Wilkie nomination allegedly a great victory. But on the other hand, I suppose I was rebelling against my parents who were Republicans so one couldn't stay a Republican.

. . .

Nobody would go into a movement which was a radical movement unless they were maladjusted—unless they came out of a family background of it. If my parents had seen socialists, or if my grandparents had been socialists, I would be a socialist because I was adjustable.

But in my own case, I'm part of a family that is military and Republican, you see. To become a pacifist and a socialist is a very clear indication of a personality maladjustment.

Or, the theory can be invoked when its applicability is not so obvious:

Well, I'll tell you the truth. I have lots of thoughts about that question, but I'm not sure what the motivating factors were. I think they were very complex rather than simple. It's true in my case, for example, that my father was an old-time socialist, although he hadn't been active in the Party from the day I was born.

Actually, he was already out of the Party from the time I was born. But generally, he was a socialist, and he used to read the *Forward* too. He read it once a week on Sunday. And he was a member of the Workmen's Circle. But he influenced me very little.

I would say the influence I got from him and from my general environment was a sort of New Dealish liberal influence that I could have absorbed completely and turned out to be a good liberal of the standard variety that we have in New York. I would never necessarily have become a socialist as a result of those influences.

I'm not a psychiatrist or a psychologist. I think there's an element— not a completely valid interpretation based on psychology, but I think there's an element in it: the revolt of the child against his parents and the problem of guilt feelings about his hostilities. In the case of the boy, it's hostility toward his father.

I wouldn't rule out these elements. I used to have a much simpler view. The older I get, the more I realize that motivation is a very complex thing for human beings. I would say that motivation is irrelevant to the validity of your views. You can be a raving madman and still be a genius.

Preoccupation with the question of motivation occurs in this generation as well as in the Interwar Generation:

The truth is that I myself would like very much to find out, and am constantly trying to find out, what motivates me to do the things that I do, and what motivated me to do the things that I did.

And I think that I can find out and still be as good a socialist as one who is in the dark as to what caused him to arrive at his views and attitudes.

It is important to emphasize again, however, that even where personal or psychological factors are believed to have been operative in the decision to become a socialist, intellectual and rational factors are given primacy in the reminiscences of all generations.

Also, regardless of how they view their own motivation in becoming socialists, disenchantment with the human capacity for rationality appears in all generations, usually in connection with the future and the possibilities of war:

If I thought that people would act rationally all the time, I would say that we won't have war. And I pray and hope and worry whether this will be the case. The difficulty is that there isn't even very much that any of us can do about it.

This I find the most frustrating part of life, living with a factor that you can't feel that you're affecting to any considerable extent.

At the same time, people like myself get active in civil rights and poverty fights and we act as if peace is going to stay because that's the only way we can act, without going crazy.

We have to assume that we're going to have a world, and that if we are, we've got to do all the things we can that will make it a decent and livable world.

Enough optimism remains, however, to make the struggle seem worthwhile:

There are rationalities. For instance, there is a willingness to give some help to rising nations—to help promote programs that have already begun.

But the terrible proneness of men to violence and the lack of progress in fighting the institution of war are the most dangerous elements.

But even that's not hopeless. If I thought it were, I'd be for the philosophy of eat, drink, and be merry, or as merry as we can, for tomorrow we die.

Political activists live in hope; they could not otherwise remain politically active. One is reminded of the myth of Sisyphus. Homer does not reveal why Sisyphus is punished by the necessity to continue in the impossible effort of rolling the stone to the top of the hill. Our Socialist Party leaders share the same punishment—a never-ending struggle. Sisyphus, however, was aware of his goal and what would comprise success; many Socialist Party leaders, in the face of repeated failures, no longer have even this source of comfort.

CHAPTER III

THE FAILURE OF
SOCIALISM IN AMERICA

A FINAL and incontestable answer to the question of why socialism and the Socialist Party failed in this country is not possible.
The very question calls forth protests such as: "The Socialist
Party failed, but socialism did not fail in America," or "Socialism
failed everywhere in the West, no more so here than in Britain
and the Scandinavian countries, which have only a nominal socialism." Or, "The Party failed politically, but not personally—it
served many valuable functions for its members."

The question of the failure of socialism in America is an ex-
ceedingly difficult one to answer, bound up as it is with values
and with present-day confusions with regard to what socialism is
as an economic system, what its goals are, and what methods
should be used for obtaining these goals:

Well, what's socialism today? So long as you don't have socialism,
it's pretty clear what you want. But once you have a little bit of
socialism, it's not so clear what you want because clarity is much
easier when you are at a distance from the thing. The outline is clearer
when you don't take in the details of what you want, and how you are
going to get it, and how you are going to manage it.

Socialism is collective ownership as opposed to private ownership,
period. What's so complicated about that? And, in the 1920s, that was
it. And into the 1930s, that was it.

Of course, the Soviet Union had their system collectivized, but we
said that's a strange animal anyhow because they had no right to make

a socialist revolution in Russia. Russia was an agricultural country, and socialism is not for pigs. Socialism is for industrial workers. So, okay, that was an accident of history.

But then, as the years have gone by, the concept of socialism was picked up all over the earth. And the use of the phrase is now universal except in the United States.

The Soviet Union has socialism. And China has socialism. But that's different. And the Scandinavian countries have socialism. That's still more different. The Labour Party of Britain is for socialism. It is the Socialist Party of Great Britain. And their socialism is a completely different animal. I am not quite sure whether they have nationalized steel or not, at this moment.

And even when the fairly conservative Catholic parties of central Europe take over, they refer to themselves as Christian Socialists.

Then Nasser is for Arab socialism. And when Castro made the revolution in Cuba, he said: "We are the first socialist republic in the Western hemisphere." And Trujillo said, "No, the Dominican Republic is."

And then you go into Southeast Asia and you have a collection of feudal lords who talk about feudal socialism. And you have a monarchic socialism and a military socialism. And you have a Socialist Party in the United States.

But we are beyond the point where it's all so clear: collectivism *vs.* private ownership. Actually, we live in a world where I suppose the majority of the peoples are living under some form of government that describes itself as more or less socialist.

So it's no longer quite so simple. And when you ask me am I still a socialist—that's a good question.

What are the basic tenets of socialism? In the final analysis, it's collectivism *vs.* private ownership. But if you were to examine any one of the societies on the face of the earth today, there is a high degree of collective action, a high degree of it.

And that includes the United States. We do it in a sneaky way in the United States, but the United States does not reject the collective action that it rejected in the early 1930s and would not even consider in the 1920s.

Given the current intricacy and complexity of economic systems, and to avoid compounding confusion, before attempting to discuss the failure of socialism in the United States, we might attempt to answer two questions. Is the United States approaching a socialist economic system? Given certain standards, how close is this country to socialism compared to other industrialized, democratic countries?

Socialism can be defined as an economic system in which there is nationalization of basic industries, a dominant public sector, equal income distribution, a total welfare state, and central economic planning. This is an ideal-typical construction. No society in existence today, whether or not it defines itself as socialist, has an economic system which meets all of the above criteria. The definition is an exaggeration of reality, containing the essential features of socialism in pure form.

Using this model as a yardstick, we must conclude that the United States is certainly not a socialist state, and whether or not it is approaching socialism is problematic.

Widespread nationalization of basic industries has not taken place in this country; floundering industries are usually subsidized, not nationalized.[1] Government policy in this country has followed the principle of encouraging private industry to undertake the production of new goods and services, rather than expand the public sector. The implementation of urban renewal programs, in which private industry has provided private housing units for middle-income groups, for the most part, is an example of the operation of this policy. The public sector is smaller in the United States than in most other industrial nations in the West. Utilities such as telephones and railways, which are state-owned in most countries, are privately owned and subject only to moderate government regulation in the United States.

Social scientists disagree in their conclusions about current trends in income distribution in the United States. A major difficulty in making accurate assessments of these trends is that data are based on reported income figures. Real income consists of actual command over goods and services by various categories of

[1] Some social critics have labeled this phenomenon "Socialism for Private Profit," or "The Rich Man's Welfare State."

people in a society. Reported income figures do not include illegal income, intrafamilial transfers of income, and fringe benefits such as hospitalization, pension benefits, deferred income payments, undistributed profits, expense accounts, etc. Higher-income groups share disproportionately in these benefits.

Given these difficulties in ascertaining real income, it is not surprising that there is disagreement among social scientists regarding trends in income distribution. Gabriel Kolko,[2] using census data on reported income, found a long-range decline in the percentage of income going to the bottom 20 per cent of American families from the years 1910 to 1959. Herman P. Miller[3] found that the percentage of national income going to the bottom 20 per cent increased up to 1944, then remained stable to 1961.

Regardless of their differences, both writers agree that the reduced income of upper-income groups, by means of progressive taxation, has been redistributed largely to middle-income groups in our society. Miller, in his cross-sectional view of national income, found that the upper 5 per cent of American families received 30 per cent of all family income in 1929 and 20 per cent of all family income in 1961. The latter figure indicates a continued substantial differential in the distribution of reported income. It should be emphasized that actual purchasing power has increased enormously within the lower strata in America over the years. However, tax cuts and loopholes, and differential access to fringe benefits have blunted the possible redistributive effects of progressive taxation considerably.

As for the other aspects of socialism, we do not have compulsory central planning or even the voluntary type of planning used in such countries as France and Belgium. Planning, by the automobile industry, for example, is short-term and is oriented toward the goals of the particular industry.

[2] Gabriel Kolko, *Wealth and Power in America* (New York: Praeger, 1962), p. 14.
[3] Herman P. Miller, *Rich Man, Poor Man* (New York: Signet Books, 1965), pp. 35–36.

Finally, the United States has a very limited welfare state compared with many European countries which have more comprehensive social security and public housing measures.

If we utilize a precise and ideal-typical definition of socialism, therefore, the question of the failure of socialism in America is a legitimate one. The literature on this question is voluminous, but agreement on the weight which should be given to various factors is rare. Reasons given for the failure of socialism range from the purely economic (the wealth of the country) to the purely ideological (the American Dream) with the purely political (the two-party electoral system) somewhere in the middle. Most analyses are multi-causal in approach, but they attempt to distinguish, arbitrarily by necessity, between primary or ultimate and secondary or contributing factors.

Occasionally in the literature, one encounters an explanation resting on a single and predominant factor. Harvey Goldberg [4] and Seymour M. Lipset and Reinhard Bendix [5] cite the American Dream as an all-important element in the failure of the socialist movement in this country. Lipset and Bendix argue that while the rate of intergenerational mobility from the working class into the middle class since the turn of the century has actually been approximately the same in various Western industrialized countries, the belief in the possibility of unlimited success for everyone has tended, in the United States, to deflect potential radical protest into transvaluational religions or into hopes for one's children. In other words, as W. I. Thomas observed, if men define situations as real, they are real in their consequences.[6]

Other examples of monistic emphasis are: the desire of immigrants in this country to become acculturated and, thus, to accept the status quo; [7] factionalism—particularly the splitting off

[4] Harvey Goldberg, *American Radicals* (New York: Monthly Review Press, 1967).

[5] Seymour M. Lipset and Reinhard Bendix, *Social Mobility in Industrial Society* (Berkeley, California: University of California Press, 1960), p. 263.

[6] W. I. Thomas and Dorothy S. Thomas, *The Child in America* (New York: Alfred A. Knopf, 1928).

[7] Wayne H. Morgan, ed., *American Socialism: 1900–1960* (New Jersey: Prentice-Hall, 1964).

from the Socialist Party of the militant Haywood group in 1912; [8] the individualism of the American national character, which was incompatible with socialist goals of collective existence; [9] the inability of the Socialist Party to reconcile its ethics with the demands of political expediency—it was "in but was not of the world";[10] and the preemption of socialist ideas by the New Deal.[11]

Examples of more complex analyses go back at least to Werner Sombart's question at the turn of the century, "Why is there no socialism in the United States?" Previously, of course, the question was phrased in terms of when socialism would arrive in the United States rather than why it did not. Karl Marx and Frederick Engels shared the unrestrained enthusiasm of the early socialists for the prospects of socialism in this country. In a letter to Friedrich Sorge, written in 1893, Engels [12] predicted that if Americans were properly informed of European theoretical knowledge of the laws of social change, their extraordinary vitality and energy could lead to victory for socialism within ten years.

Werner Sombart, writing some ten years later, anticipated the thousands of pages which were to be written in the years to follow on the question of why socialism did not arrive in the United States. Sombart [13] attributed the failure of the movement, up to that time, to the fluidity of the class structure in the United States, to the open frontier which contributed to this fluidity, and to the economic wealth and rising standards of living in this country.

[8] Ira Kipnis, *The American Socialist Movement: 1897–1912* (New York: Columbia University Press, 1952).

[9] Donald Drew Egbert, "Socialism and American Art," in Donald D. Egbert and Stow Persons, eds., *Socialism and American Life* (Princeton, New Jersey: Princeton University Press, 1952), p. 621.

[10] Daniel Bell, "Marxian Socialism in American Life," *Ibid.*, p. 217.

[11] Ralph Milliband and John Saville, *The Socialist Register* (New York: Monthly Review Press, 1964).

[12] Karl Marx and Frederick Engels, *Letters to Americans* (New York: International Publishers, 1953), p. 141.

[13] Werner Sombart, *Why Is There No Socialism in the United States?* (Tubingen, Germany: J. C. B. Mohr [Paul Siebeck], 1906).

Selig Perlman attributed the failure of cooperative momements in the United States to the fluidity of the class structure—"the opportunity for the exceptional workman to desert his class and set up in business for himself," [14] to the ethnic and racial cleavages which prevented class solidarity and consciousness of kind from developing in this country, and to certain aspects of American national character which were incompatible with cooperative social organization: the traditional individualism in this country and the heritage of puritanism with its emphasis on individual achievement.

More recently, G. D. H. Cole [15] singled out the political democracy which existed in this country in contrast to Europe, where workers found a common rallying ground in opposition to autocracy and militarism. He believed that a second factor preventing the continued growth of the movement in America was the cleavage, reinforced by ethnic differences, between skilled and unskilled workers.

Typically, those analysts who maintain a traditional Marxist orientation attribute the failure of the socialist movement in this country to economic factors—next to which all other factors are viewed as secondary or derivative. [16]

REASONS FOR FAILURE

When our respondents were asked to give their opinion on this problem, they replied with lengthy and often scholarly arguments, indicating in many instances an extraordinary memory for facts and figures and a thorough familiarity with the history of the movement. Those leaders who have written about the socialist movement and its failures in this country tend to repeat the

---

[14] Selig Perlman, *A History of Trade Unionism in the United States* (New York: The Macmillan Co., 1922), p. 65.

[15] G. D. H. Cole, *The History of Socialist Thought* (London: Macmillan and Co., 1955).

[16] Paul M. Sweezey, "The Influence of Marxian Economics on American Thought and Practice," Donald D. Egbert and Stow Persons, eds., *Socialism and American Life*, p. 453.

arguments which have already appeared in print. There have been no major changes in the thinking of these leaders about the problem.

Content analysis of the data indicates only the relative frequencies with which certain factors are mentioned. It does not reveal the relative emphasis or weighting given to these factors nor does it reveal the evaluation of these factors by our respondents. For example, the New Deal economic reforms mentioned by two respondents as a factor in the failure of the movement can, in one case, be viewed as the realization of the goals of the Socialist Party (at least in terms of its immediate goals) or, in another case, as a conservative holding action on the part of the ruling class in this country.

In general, patterns in the thinking of the leaders about the problem of the failure of socialism in America do not coincide with generational categories in that no one factor is cited more frequently by one generation than another. However, there is a tendency for certain factors to be given more weight in particular generations. All of the leaders give multiple reasons for the failure of the movement.

The most frequently mentioned reason for the failure of the movement and the Party in this country is the New Deal reforms and other economic reforms that have been introduced over the past fifty years. In descending order, other frequently cited reasons are: factionalism and splitting within the Party; the failure to capture the imagination of the labor movement, or stated in another way, the inapplicability of socialist ideology to the goals and desires of the working class in this country; the fluidity of the class structure and the relative weakness of the class struggle in this country; the two-party electoral system; ethnic differences and cleavages; and the fact that the ideology was imported from Europe.

Causes mentioned infrequently but with about equal frequency are: the wealth of the nation; the American Dream; the poor leadership of the Party; governmental repression of the Party and its pacifist stand on war.

Significantly, there are a large number of miscellaneous and infrequent responses such as: Americans like to remain with the winner; the Party did not have enough morale; the American Labor Party outmaneuvered the Party; confusion existed in the public mind between communism and socialism; and socialism was a Jewish movement, and in the United States Jewish political movements are not subject to great growth.

EVALUATIONS OF FAILURE

At least since the time of Edmund Burke, in the realm of political theory, and at least since the time of Otto von Bismarck, in the realm of political action, it has been recognized that the essence of conservatism is timely reform. Our respondents tend to affirm this, although not consistently in those terms. Almost all of the leaders, with very few exceptions, list the New Deal reforms and other economic reforms, going back to the Progressive Era, as a decisive factor in the failure of the socialist movement in this country. The evaluation of the adequacy of these reforms varies, however, and usually it tends to coincide with the present relationship of our respondents to the Socialist Party.

Leaders who left the Party many years ago tend to emphasize the material and moral gains that have been achieved in this country since the days of early, unregulated capitalism:

We are not satisfied, naturally, and we want more change and more rapid change. But you must remember how things *have* changed.

There is less corruption and graft in government. There is less violence against minority groups and against labor. There is less flagrant bias in the newspapers (people are smarter). And business methods, while they leave much to be desired, are certainly less ruthless than they were.

. . .

In the new countries all over the world, socialism is taken for granted. In this country, there has been a conscious campaign, a concerted effort of all the opinion makers to isolate America from Europe. They don't want to share this European general acceptance of the ideals of socialism.

However, as far as the practical development of socialist measures is concerned, America is an advanced socialist country. In terms of national control—national, government control of the direction of the economy and the practical distribution of its fruits, the increasing distribution of profits to the masses—socialism is here.

. . .

Basically, socialism means collectivism versus private ownership. Well, today we have a high degree of collectivism in the United States.

First of all, we have collective restraints on industry. The minimum wage law is a collective restraint, so that you may not pay a wage below a certain level. Now, it's private ownership and it's called private ownership, but it's no longer the private ownership in the sense that it once was, when you could do any damn thing you wanted to do with your property. That's no longer valid.

The fact that you now have a National Labor Relations Act that says that when the majority of your workers want to join the union, you *must* bargain with them, you must recognize them is a tremendous restraint on ownership. It means that you own it, but you are limited.

And there are other forms of collective action—unemployment insurance, workmen's compensation, social security, and, now, we're moving into the whole field of medicine.

The original socialist concept didn't *just* mean governmental ownership; it called for a variety of collective activities whereby people cooperatively would pool their funds and their knowhow in order to accomplish certain purposes.

In the 1930s, the Union Health Center was a freak. It was a form of third-party medicine run by the ILGWU. Today, third party medicine probably covers the majority of the people in this country. You either have Group Health or HIP or Blue Shield or Blue Cross, or you are under some veterans' plan or under some military plan, or under some other municipal or governmental employees plan, or under some union-run plan. Well, this is a form of collective protection for the community; it's a form of collectivism.

But we really go much beyond that. You take housing in the United States. You take the whole FHA program, the whole GI housing program, the whole Title One program, and federal and state and municipal monies for low-cost housing. Government housing—it runs into billions of dollars in the United States. It's government *housing*.

Once, housing was something that belonged to landlords exclusively. And now there's huge government housing, even though it may appear to be private. For instance, if you have an FHA mortgage, it's government underwritten. Fundamentally, it's the government that's financing the housing except that the government says to you, "If you get an FHA mortgage, you may go to the bank and the bank will lend you the money at a given rate of interest. And we will insure that mortgage. In other words, if you can't pay, we will pay."

Now really, this is the government saying, "We are putting up the housing. We stand behind it." It's socialism at six per cent, and the bank gets its cut of this kind of socialism.

The socialists also believed that there should be a program enacted immediately short of socialism that would provide a whole series of social insurances and securities. And the socialists, when they used to campaign everywhere in the world, didn't just talk about socialism, they spoke about minimum wages and social security and the rest of it.

Well, that we have. We got it in what was called the New Deal. It's an expanding concept however. It isn't just the original New Deal. It's the New Deal plus everything that's come along on top of the New Deal. All the other things.

So this aspect of socialism we've accepted, even in the United States. What else was socialism? Socialism was a concept of the role of labor in society. This was the whole notion of industrial democracy. That is, the working man should have a voice, an important voice, in (a) the economy and in (b) the government of the nation.

And the old socialist concept was very simple. A government was a class government. The capitalists owned and called all the industrial shots, and the capitalists also owned the government. It was their government, and, therefore, you had to have a class party to dispossess it.

Well, you cannot say that the American worker does not have a sizable voice, a dominant voice—surely it's not the only voice and I'm not sure that it's the major voice, but it's a sizable voice in determining the nature of the economy. Surely, this is true in the area of wages, but more than that in many other areas.

And politically, it's no longer possible to say that this is simply the government of the capitalists and that the working man has no voice in the government of the nation. Of course, he has a voice. It's perfectly obvious.

We are constantly being told by right-wing critics that Johnson is nothing but the tool of labor, and so was Truman and so was Roosevelt. It's not true. They are not the tool of labor. And it's not true—as some of them charge—that the moment the labor bosses speak, all the congressmen jump. It's not true.

However, labor has a very important political voice in the United States at the present time, and, more important in terms of the future, labor can have a *greater* political voice. As a matter of fact, it's just a matter of educating its own ranks and organizing to do a better job.

So the old socialist notion that it's important to have an industrial democracy—I think it's happening. I don't think we have *the* industrial democracy, but we have been moving every year in the direction of industrial democracy in the United States *and* in the direction of political democracy.

We have not achieved a full victory. We may not achieve a full victory ever. I'm not sure we want a full victory. But certainly this has been the direction. This is clear. . . .

In a general sense, the acceptance by the society of responsibility for the economic well-being of the individual—there is no country on the face of the earth today that does not accept this to a greater or to a lesser degree. We have really turned our back completely on the notion of everybody for himself.

Now, is this socialism? Well, it's socialism of a sort. But who has the other kind of socialism, except in the Soviet-run countries? Otherwise you don't have it. Hitler, in a sense, had it, and he practically took over the whole show. And Peron came mighty close to it.

If you just see socialism as a diagram, that is, government ownership, it only exists really in the Soviet countries. In other countries, we have socialism or semi-socialism in the form of collectivism. And the old concept of what socialism is today is *out*.

Socialism, we see again, now means many different things to different people.

The leaders who are still members of the Socialist Party tend to evaluate welfare state measures in this country and governmental regulations of industry as inadequate—too little, if not too late:

As far as socialism and socialist ideas are concerned, there certainly was a different attitude toward a good many things that the socialists preached in the early days than you find at present.

When the Socialist Party was first born, only a minority of Americans was in favor of social legislation—of unemployment insurance, old-age pensions, health insurance. Only a minority felt that the government had any interest in doing anything about the elimination of the slums and in the bringing about of decent housing.

There was much less emphasis on education, particularly on higher education. There was much less control and regulation of the great industries of the country. We just didn't have the public ownership that we have at the present time—in the TVA and the electrical industry. And the concept of the welfare state was a concept which seemed to be alien to the American people.

I remember in 1929 coming back from Vienna after having seen any number of very fine homes for the workers in Vienna, and the slums disappearing, and urging that we do the same thing in the United States. And my audiences said, "Well, that's a fine thing, but it's not a function of government."

Well, in 1936 and 1937, it became a function of government, and we have advanced quite a distance, although the great problem is still to be solved.

If you go down to Washington now and hear what they say about it's being a government job to eliminate poverty—that's a far cry from what one heard at the beginning of the century.

The trade union movement has grown from two or three million to about seventeen million. And now there are any number of laws protecting the movement, whereas at the turn of the century, one heard simply of injunctions and police brutality, and so forth, preventing the legitimate activities of the labor movement.

So there has been quite a different attitude toward what a community should do in protecting the workers, in abolishing poverty, in developing public agencies, education, recreation, and things of that sort.

However, we socialists would say that *still* you find the great and unjust inequality of wealth that one found at the beginning of the century. *Still* you find tremendous concentration of control in American industry—the development of monopolies and oligarchies and so forth.

Still you find, on the whole, the motive of success is that of becoming rich rather than serving the community. *Still* you find five million people unemployed. *Still* you find one-fifth of the people in bad homes.

Still you find, with the tremendous development of technology, that social legislation has not kept pace. *Still* you find our natural resources are being wasted. We are not doing the job in preserving our resources —our forests, our waterways. *Still* you find billions of dollars lost every year for lack of flood control.

Still you find, say in communications, the great cities of the country are lacking railroad communications because the private railroads don't find it profitable to have proper commuter services. *Still* you find chaos as far as transportation and communication is concerned, and so forth.

Of course, the socialists were incorrect in timing social change. They were incorrect in feeling that the capitalist system did not have before it, the opportunity to expand as it has expanded. They had little idea of the tremendous development of productivity as a result of our greatly advanced technology. And they probably had little concept of what taxation could do in giving a tremendous resource to the government through income and inheritance taxes, and so forth.

But with the development of technology, it becomes more and more necessary to have national economic planning. And we have only the beginning of national economic planning.

And the need for democratic social planning, which the socialists have urged, is as great if not greater than before.

GENERATIONAL PERSPECTIVES

As I have pointed out, no striking differences arise between the generations in the relative frequency with which particular reasons for the failure of the Party or the movement are singled out. However, there is a tendency for emphasis on particular factors to vary. Those which are emphasized tend to be related to the social conditions prevailing in America at the time of most active participation in the movement by the different generations.

The World War I Generation, particularly those who were born in Europe, tend to stress the fluidity of the class structure, and the ease of vertical social mobility in this country:

When I used to teach history classes, I would say, "Look, if you want to see the difference between the labor movement in the United Kingdom and here, there are two points that you must understand."

The worker, the dissatisfied worker in the city, dissatisfied with his treatment as a worker, had an alternative in America. He could take off. The brainy worker went West instead of going into socialism. "Go West, young man." There was land here, you see.

There was opportunity here. Education wasn't so caste bound. Here you didn't get the whole caste system that you had in England.

I don't know whether I sound ancient, but in England when I was a child in the early 1900s, we used to sing in our church school, "The Rich Man in His Castle, The Poor Man at His Gate, God Made Them, High or Lowly, and Ordered Their Estate."

That is, you were born there and you would *stay* there. And this caste system in Europe was not present here. After the Americans destroyed the American Indians—bumped them off, or put them up safely in reservations—there was no "squirearchy" here.

As a matter of fact, the attempt to introduce the feudal system down in Virginia failed because the people they brought over to be serfs went off and got land for themselves. There was always the frontier factor present here.

I'm not suggesting that people went out and picked up the Kohinoor diamond or things of that sort, although some people actually did that. But there were opportunities here. There was almost a blank tablet on which people could write.

And so, the vigorous, militant worker—he found satisfaction in going out and becoming Andrew Carnegie rather than being Eugene Debs.

That is the American Dream. You can call anybody by his first name after you've known them for a few days. You do not bow or curtsy because this guy supposedly has got blue blood or he is a lord or a lady or something of that sort.

That is the essence of the American Dream: that a man can stand upright and be a man and not have to "kowtow" to his superiors.

If a man felt irreligious, he could be irreligious—like Ingersoll. If he wanted to talk like Walt Whitman, he could do it. You were away from your cultured, manicured, ancient traditional society.

These are all circumstances which were more important than the socialist idealism that the immigrants brought, because even if they still held to it as a sort of nostalgic dream, their sons and daughters didn't.

Their sons and daughters went to college. They got better jobs and they engaged in businesses of their own or they found employment in the corporations—and things of that sort.

The Interwar Generation tends to regard New Deal Reforms and the electoral difficulties of third parties in this country as basic factors in the failure of the Party:

I would say that the socialist movement found a number of obstacles in its path as a result of the political system in this country. This was particularly a result of the fact that every four years you were fighting primarily for the election of a president rather than concentrating more on the election of various congressmen from various parts of the country.

This is what you have in Great Britain and some other countries. In Great Britain, for instance, the Prime Minister is elected by members of the Party who are members of Parliament and not by the people as a whole.

In the United States, every four years, it seems to be largely a contest between say Kennedy on the one hand, Goldwater on the other—between presidential candidates—and in many states, a few votes might mean a difference in a large number of electoral votes.

In New York, for instance, a few votes for the Republicans or the Democrats might mean that—what is it, seventy-two votes—seventy-two electoral votes might swing one way or another.

Consequently, throughout the history of political parties in the United States you find that people in every state were saying, "Now, shall I throw my vote away on a minority party, a minority candidate? If I do, I might be instrumental in electing the worst of the two candidates."

They would say, "Yes, I believe in socialism and I don't think there is much difference between the Republican and Democratic Party, but there is some difference, and I want to cast my vote in such a way as to make it possible for the more liberal or the less illiberal of the two major candidates to be elected rather than to increase the vote of the socialist candidates."

Therefore, when there has been such a concentration on presidential candidates in the two parties, it has been difficult oftentimes for a socialist candidate to get a vote that is in proportion to his real acceptance by the American people.

It was so in the case of Norman Thomas, time and time again. People said, "Well, Norman Thomas is the best candidate among the three, but if I vote for him it may be that the Republicans will get in, will obtain the electoral votes in my particular state. Therefore, I will not take a chance. I will vote for the lesser of two evils instead."

That has been to a considerable extent, I think, responsible for the many thousands of votes that the socialists have lost in presidential campaigns.

• • •

I would say that the fact of the two-party electoral system in this country was first in importance in the failure of the Party. I'd say that even if Roosevelt had *not* taken our policies, we would not have been successful in becoming a mass party.

No third party can succeed. Even the Republican Party when it started out was a second party. It was built on the collapse of the Whigs.

And this is something about the American political scene that I think a lot of historians have not really recognized. For instance, Danny Bell, in his analysis of the decline of the Socialist Party, talks about the "program was in but not of this world."

Well, it's nonsense because everything that he said about the Socialist Party in the United States applied equally to the Socialist Party in France, in the Scandinavian countries, the labor parties or social democratic parties, the British Labour Party. The same kinds of compromises had to be made there. You had the same problems of factionalism within the parties. You had the right wings and the left wings.

The difference is that in a party in those countries where, by use of the parliamentary system, there was a chance of victory, that chance of victory is a cementing force that keeps these factional disputes from becoming splits.

In a situation where there is no possibility of electoral victory in that way, then doctrinal purity becomes the *sine qua non* and you have splits.

The World War II Generation, having come of political age in a period of prosperity, tends to stress the economic wealth of the United States—its natural resources and the great pace and scope of industrial expansion:

That's a very big question. So far as I'm concerned, I'm never satisfied that I know the answer to the question of why socialism failed in America.

I think there can be no question that the basic objective answer or the basic answer lies in objective circumstances rather than in party tactics.

And that objective factor has been the phenomenal capacity of capitalism in America to satisfy human wants and needs. I think we socialists vastly underestimated the ability of capitalism to be as productive, as flexible, as successful as it has been, whether you look at the classical Marxian analysis or the non-Marxian socialists.

You pick up the old socialist material from pre-World War I days, and you will find that inevitably all of them took the position that the doom of capitalism was around the corner. Capitalism simply could not survive. It couldn't meet the needs of the people. It couldn't expand. It was doomed and its end was only a matter of a short number of years. Debs repeated this over and over again in his speeches.

Well, I think history has proved that they were absolutely wrong in this respect. This is not my own theory. Obviously, it's a very common one. And I think that's the most important factor to understand in the failure of socialism as a political force in the United States.

Workers were not convinced that a change in the system was necessary in order to provide them with the things that they needed. On the contrary, they were convinced that within the system they could get the things that they needed, and from the standpoint of what they thought they needed they were *right*.

After all, as a democrat, I can't impose my view of what they need on theirs. They were right and the socialists were wrong.

The workers said, when it comes to pork chops, they could get everything they wanted from their own standpoint—which I regard as a narrow and limited one—under the capitalist system, through their unions, through the old American Federation of Labor, and its business unionism.

And history proves that they were right. That doesn't mean that my socialist goal is not a valid one—that it's not a correct ideal toward which to work. But it does prove that the socialist economic analysis of those days was an incorrect one.

Now you can't build a powerful mass movement based only on putting forward the ideals of a finer, more moral, or more upright social order.

The fact is, as far as I know, never in history has a mass movement that has involved tens of thousands and millions of people been based simply on a vision of a better society without the prod of misery behind it.

And workers in America weren't miserable, although it's true there were ups and downs. Still, each subsequent up was higher than the previous up. So they always had the feeling that with a little more effort, with some more savings, with some breaks, they would be able to make out. And by and large, they did.

This is what basically accounts for the difference between the socialist movement in this country, politically, and the European socialist movements.

Incidentally, if you look at the Socialist Party in the United States before World War I and compare it with the Labour Party in Britain, you'll find they were pretty much the same.

In 1912, we had over a thousand elected public officials, a couple of members in Congress, members in state legislatures, city councils, and so on; and the British Labour Party wasn't much ahead of us.

Likewise, in terms of our influence in the trade union movement. In 1912, we got one-third of the vote of the delegates to the AFL convention, and the trade unions of Britain had not yet fully endorsed the Labour Party or socialism. That didn't come actually until the end of World War I.

But the United States benefited economically from World War I. Britain was hurt by it, although not as much as by the Second World War. We proved in World War I that American capitalism could produce guns and butter in increasing quantities. There was no conflict between the two. It could produce more and more butter, and more and more guns at the same time.

And that, in my opinion, was the basic historical factor—the objective factor.

IT DID NOT FAIL

As I stated in Chapter I, expectations that the Socialist Party would be successful were never high in the World War II Generation, and belief in the inevitability of socialism was no longer the all-encompassing faith that it had been for members of the older generations, particularly the World War I Generation. Leon Festinger, in his study of a social movement, found that an individual with a strong belief, who has taken irrevocable actions because of it, when presented with undeniable and unequivocal evidence that his belief is wrong, will emerge not only unshaken but even more convinced of his beliefs than ever before.[17]

Over half of the leaders in the World War I Generation believe that socialism as a social movement did not fail in this country. A few leaders in the Interwar Generation also have this belief. No leader in the World War II Generation expresses this conviction. There would seem to be a relationship between the strength of the initial belief in inevitability and the need to claim success for these beliefs and goals by the different generations. One way to reduce the dissonance of an awareness of a disparity between goals sought and goals achieved is to emphasize the latter.

The failure of socialism in this country is viewed by many of the older leaders as a matter of degree and a matter of definition. No one denies the failure of the Socialist Party as a political organization, but there are varying estimates of the Party's effect on the centers of political power in this country and on the general moral climate in America. The older leaders argue that the New Deal utilized Socialist Party platforms as a source for its measures of economic reform. But, as I remarked earlier, those who are still members of the Party are more indignant about what remains to be done:

I've been addressing myself to the question of the failure of the Socialist Party organizationally. But, you see, one of the things that damaged the Party organizationally was the fact that much of its

17 Leon Festinger, Henry W. Riecken, Stanley Schachter, eds., *When Prophesy Fails* (New York: Harper & Row, 1964), p. 3.

ideology—at least the tone and temper of its ideology—finally prevailed.

The key element that attracted me into the Socialist Party—the idea of social responsibility for the welfare of the individual in a society in which such interdependence exists that no man's success is wholly of his own making, and no man's defeat is wholly his own defeat—that idea of social responsibility became the singularly attractive thing about the socialist movement. And that idea *did* prevail.

One of the premises of the socialist movement—namely that economic conditions would produce changes in attitudes—proved to be true. The depression had a remarkable effect on the American outlook.

And there is no doubt that the New Deal administration came into office with no program. All you've got to do is look at the platform of the Democratic Party 1932.

The Democratic Party had no program, but it cast around for a program and the only program that was available was the Socialist Party platform.

I think it would be a very interesting part of your study to look at the legislation that was adopted in the 1930s and stack it up against the program of immediate demands contained in the Socialist Party platform of 1928 for example, or '32.

Now, having proved successful to this extent, if I were a young fellow coming on the scene in 1936 or in 1944, when my political judgments were being formed for the first time, and if my initial motivation was the acceptance by society of social responsibility, I would have been attracted to the New Deal.

But, I think there is more to be added. The New Deal, while it adopted these things and helped to cushion the shocks of the depression by meeting the socialist immediate demands, actually failed as an economic program. It did not solve the unemployment problem. The war did.

Now, that's a hell of an alternative solution to the solution that socialists were offering for solving the unemployment problem.

Not only the acceptance of the principle of social responsibility and the enactment of specific measures of economic reform but other, less tangible benefits are believed by some of the older leaders to be directly attributable to the efforts of the Socialist Party in this country:

The idea of human solidarity is something with which I think the socialists are still ahead of their time. I go around talking, these days, when I'm invited, about one world or none. If we don't hang together, we will hang separately.

That was as good an argument for this country in 1776 as it is in the world of 1970, and with all the economic implications that it involves.

And this is why I am, to a certain extent, an unreconstructed socialist—as far as the basic ideals go. I still think that what the socialist movement did was a wonderful educational job. It built up ideals. It did not achieve electoral success, but the ideas that it developed, the methods of tackling social problems that it developed, have become part and parcel of the system of our time.

So is that failure? I don't think so. And it is just gross miseducation and misunderstanding that prevents the ordinary people from seeing this.

Others argue that the Party served as a valuable training ground for many people who went on to become important figures in public life:

I have come to the conclusion that in some mysterious way, our movement developed talent in a way which was fantastically out of proportion to its size; or else we drew to ourselves people who were, by their personal abilities, destined to play important roles.

Let me put it this way. In my present job I have the opportunity of meeting many times with the representatives of community and national groups interested in—well it starts with civil rights, but it spreads from that to many social and community issues.

Cutting across the whole range from trade union representatives to Protestant and Catholic church representatives, we can pick out maybe half the people participating as people whom we knew personally—knew as part of that infinitesimal socialist group. People that participated.

Oh, and I want to say, cutting across from labor to religion, I left out the academic world where this is equally true.

Recently I went to a certain well-known graduate school, and I met the new dean. And I knew him, by God. He was one of the best street corner orators we had in our Socialist Party branch.

The leaders recognize a disparity between the ethical ideals of the movement and the conditions which exist in contemporary society but:

As far as the ideals that we preached, I think they had great success in America. Look what's happening. Look what's happened in fifty years.

People eventually find out what their interests are. I must say that socialist ideals didn't come the way we expected. Nothing comes the way founders expect, not even religion.

Moses couldn't get into Israel or Palestine. Things switch. Things have a terrific way of being different from expectations. Christ had the same experience.

Every preacher of high ideals finds that when an ideal becomes part of the mass, it changes in form. But if you look at it sensibly, part of your heritage is included.

So I wouldn't say that socialism was a failure. The role of liberalism comes from our people—people who were trained by us, first, second, and third generation. Somehow or other it has a way of sticking. It comes down from the father.

And yet:

The immediate demands of the Socialist Party platform consisted of what we already have today. And I don't think it would be out of place to say that we have left our contribution—the contribution of the Socialist Party toward the realization of social security and things like that.

The workers earn a decent wage and they have comforts—good housing. In my day, bathroom facilities were down in the yard. The bedrooms had no windows. And one room served as dining room, living room, and additional sleeping space.

The workers don't have this kind of world today. That was something we had to work for and fight for and bleed for. They don't have to do it today. They have it on a silver platter—without fighting, without striking, without being sent to jail, without policemen's clubs. They get the things they need and want without any struggle.

Well, we didn't. We had to fight for these things and fight hard, and, therefore . . . as I said in the beginning, it's a different world. I think we gained materially enormously . . . but maybe we lost something spiritually, too.

What has been lost spiritually, perhaps, is the belief in unlimited progress and the perfectibility of man. This belief is dead now, and this is the broader, symbolic meaning of the "God is Dead" thesis.

With the possible exception of a few idiosyncratic responses, each of the various factors mentioned by the leaders as contributing to the failure of the socialist movement in this country undoubtedly had an important effect. They can all be subsumed under the three general categories of explanation mentioned in the beginning of this chapter: the economic, the political, and the ideological. In reality, these three types of explanatory factors have operated inseparably, reinforcing and reacting upon each other; in retrospect, they cannot be assigned ultimate, intermediate, and immediate causal significance with any degree of assurance.

Regardless of how they feel about the success or failure of socialism in America, almost all of our respondents continue to define themselves as socialists. Even those who are most enthusiastic about the economic changes that have occurred in this country are not quite satisfied. What is it that they still desire, and do they feel it can be achieved?

CHAPTER IV

THE FUTURE OF
SOCIALISM IN AMERICA

PREDICTING the future of the American economy and of American society is a task that many of the leaders undertook very reluctantly and with the greatest uneasiness. Replies to the question of the future of socialism in America involved a summing up and setting forth of their present purposes and future hopes.

The responses often were ambiguous, evasive, and inconsistent, if not actually contradictory. The data were extremely difficult to code into clear-cut, mutually exclusive categories for purposes of analysis. Protests such as, "It's very hard to know; my crystal ball isn't working," and "When I was younger, I used to do a lot of predicting, but now I hate to do it" were common in the younger generations. The World War I Generation is less uncomfortable about their present definition of socialism, and much less uncertain about the future of socialism.

Only a few leaders in the two younger generations believe that socialism, however they presently define it, is inevitable. On the other hand, a majority of the World War I Generation leaders believe that socialism in one form or another is inevitable in America. This generation is much less apt to feel that socialism is anachronistic.

The loss of certainty, particularly by the younger leaders, is in distinct contrast to the belief in inevitability which prevailed in the early days of the socialist movement.

A brief sampling of published statements by leaders of the Party in the 1920s and 1930s, illustrates this early optimism:

I am hopeful of seeing a great and powerful, perhaps even a triumphant socialist movement in this country in my own days.[1]

. . .

There can be no communism except through socialism, which must follow capitalism as the dawn follows the night.[2]

. . .

As a socialist, I have always striven to pave the way for the next step forward in human progress, convinced that the selfish system of capitalism could not endure; a prop here or there may stave off its final collapse, but the end is inevitable. When that comes, what have we to take its place? Surely we need not go through bloody revolution, anarchy, and chaos to reach the goal of human happiness. Socialism is the only sane, peaceful, and honorable way toward it. If I did not think so, I would not be a socialist. I am just as sure of it in these dark days as I ever was in the past. I still hold that if a thing is worth doing, It Can Be Done.[3]

The original certainty about the future of socialism persists largely for the oldest respondents:

You see, I believe there is a great future in the United States for the socialist movement, and, I believe, under *that* name. Although the name was stolen by the National Socialists and by this and that, it is *still* a very respectable name in the mind of the masses. Even in America.

In other countries, it is the *great* name.

I believe that democracy without socialism cannot exist. And nobody has convinced me that we have to change the name socialism.

It has been a label for one hundred years. Owen was a socialist; the Jesuits had a socialist state. The name is a valuable property which we should use and not forget.

[1] Morris Hillquit, *Loose Leaves From a Busy Life* (New York: Rand School Press, 1932), p. 330.

[2] David Karsner, *Talks With Debs* (New York, New York Call, 1922), p. 65.

[3] James Maurer, *It Can Be Done* (New York: Rand School Press, 1938), pp. 321–22.

I believe that students, especially, get a tremendous uplift out of the idea that there is something like socialism. It'a a tremendous hope for people who see what is going on in the world.

I believe it is wrong to start a new movement. The socialist movement has thousands of martyrs who died in the name of socialism—who were shot in Russia and were hanged in Austria. They will *not* be forgotten.

Historical memories die hard for some members of this generation.

The younger generations, however, with few exceptions, do not share this certainty and do not see socialism as inevitable:

I think that there are so many pitfalls that lie along the way, that other solutions might gain acceptance. I'd hate to see that happen.

I think that there are real dangers—this is due to the advance of technology—that some type of native American fascism may be the answer to the problems that are accumulating now. So, I'm not predicting inevitable victory.

. . .

At this point, I would not predict what will be the state of affairs twenty-five years from now.

One of the psychological strengths of Marxism—the psychological strength of any religion has this—was that there was an inevitability about it. "History is on our side. What we believe in is going to come to pass, because regardless of what we do, history is going to make come to pass."

Well, I never believed that. I don't believe it now. I think it's up for grabs.

Before discussing their beliefs about the future of the movement in this country, the leaders were asked to describe their present conception of socialism. They also discussed their position on the means which should be employed for achieving their present political and economic goals; what they regard as the most serious problem facing American society today; and their opinion of the New Left.

PRESENT CONCEPTIONS OF SOCIALISM

The majority of our respondents no longer include government ownership of productive resources in their present conception of socialism. There are generational differences in this respect, however. The World War I Generation is more apt to have retained the traditional definition than the two younger generations.

Most of the leaders currently conceive of socialism as consisting of central planning and government regulation of basic industries or they conceive of socialism as consisting primarily of nonmaterial, intangible goals, such as human solidarity and brotherhood, respect for human integrity, and the full utilization of potential creativity in the society.

The full acceptance by society of the principle of social responsibility for the fate of all its citizens or of greater commitment and democratic participation by all citizens are other examples of nonspecific and idealistic definitions of socialism.

The leaders who now emphasize ethical or spiritual goals in their present conceptions of socialism are almost all in the World War I Generation. Very few leaders in the two younger generations specify these kinds of goals in their present definitions of socialism. This is evidence of the progressive decline in idealism or, certainly, greater unwillingness to verbalize idealism in the younger generations.

There are two female respondents in our sample. They both emphasize intangible, nonmaterial humanistic goals in their present conceptions of socialism, evidence perhaps of their extension of the integrative, expressive aspects of the feminine role in our society to the realm of politics.

Those leaders who no longer believe that government ownership of basic industries is necessary, or desirable, give as the reason for the change in their thinking the fact of the managerial revolution:

I don't think we can talk any longer in terms of the nineteenth-century phrases—one of which was the class struggle. Nor can we talk any longer in terms of simple nationalization.

We still have to talk in terms of planning, but I think we have a much greater knowledge of the mechanisms of planning than we ever had before. And, in addition, we have a technology, the computer, which makes planning very feasible.

I think the principal things that I, at any rate, learned, or think I learned out of wartime economics, was that you don't have to have government owning in order to be able to exercise control. We had a whole priority system under which the government was able to influence the channeling of products in different directions.

We used to think that the only way you could plan was to take industry out of the hands of the owner. Today we know that even owners don't control their enterprises.

There's a central management class which has far greater influence over the decisions of enterprises than the owners, in many cases.

The argument that technically trained managers have taken over industry from owners and that managers, by virtue of their skills, rationality and (presumed) decreased proprietary interest in their firms, are more amenable to government control and considerations of public interest, presents certain difficulties.[4]

Managers tend to own stocks in the corporations in which they are employed.[5] They usually take advantage of stock options. They are in a position to have early knowledge of events likely to influence the price of securities issued by the corporations which employ them. And they are controlled (hired or fired) by boards of directors who own stocks in the corporations.

Despite recent public-service ventures such as job-training programs, the goal of private industry, whether operated by robber barons or rationally recruited managers is still to maximize

---

[4] See, James Burnham, *The Managerial Revolution* (Bloomington, Indiana: University Press, 1960, first published in 1941). Burnham, a disillusioned ex-Marxist, argued that the managerial class would displace the propertied class and become the ruling class of the future in industrial societies.

[5] For an excellent discussion of the relationship between the control of corporations and the ownership of stock, see G. William Domhoff, *Who Rules America?* (Englewood Cliffs, New Jersey: Prentice-Hall, Inc., 1967), Chapter II.

profits. Failure to act in the public interest can be justified by managers as due to stockholder disapproval of nonprofitable activities. The unwillingness to locate plants in urban ghetto areas has been defended recently on these grounds by some managers of large firms.

Another argument advanced by leaders who no longer desire government ownership of basic industries, is that government ownership endangers the democratic process:

I have some doubts as to whether I want the government to own everything. I didn't have doubts when I was younger; I have *very real* doubts now.

I have doubts because the years have gone by and I have developed less and less faith in human beings, and I don't want power concentrated anywhere.

I am afraid of a concentration of power. I am not talking a cheap Republican states' right talk. I just feel safer if I know that there are many conflicting forces in the United States able to challenge one another. Then I think democracy is a little bit safe.

I have lived now in enough organizations and have watched politics and economics closely in world affairs—sufficiently closely—to feel that if you have one organization owning everything and you have one political party, of necessity, in control of that ownership, inside of that party you are going to have a dominant caucus.

And inside of that you are going to have an inner circle to run the caucus. And what you end up with is an outrageous kind of dictatorship that controls everything.

It isn't like the old theocracies which controlled your religious life— it controls your thinking, it controls your voting, it controls your *job!* And once you're fired, that's it. You don't just lose your job. You've lost your life. Capital punishment.

So I have very serious doubts as to whether I favor all-out collective ownership. What is more, watching the American scene and the development of the American economy, I'm not so sure we need it.

One of the big arguments in favor of collective ownership is that it is the only answer to recurrent depressions that would ultimately produce unemployment of such magnitude as to bring the entire economy to a standstill.

And in 1929 it happened—it was very close to happening. It has been happening less and less. We have not had a depression of such magnitude since 1929. Our depressions have not been getting worse.

As a matter of fact, we have reason to believe that if we had a liberal congress, which we really haven't had, and a liberal-minded president of the United States, and a trade union push, and a few other things, we could probably get full employment in the United States *without* socialism.

I am not quite sure I want to risk all the dangers and possible tyrannies of a socialist society in the old sense. I want labor as an independent force. I want social legislation. I want restraints on industry. I wouldn't hesitate to nationalize certain industries, if that is the best way of dealing with a particular problem.

And I think we could lick poverty. We can lick ignorance. We can lick disease. It's true that some people would still be exploiting other people. It's true. And you kind of resent it.

And I just say, "Well, but suppose we stop all this exploiting by turning everything over to the government. What are the negatives on that one?" And you are hesitant.

And so, you sort of strike the middle ground.

I would say that people who, in the past, would have been socialists of the doctrinaire and dogmatic variety that I and many others represented in the 1930s, living in the 1960s and confronted by all these facts, say, "Well, who needs that kind of doctrinaire socialist? In fact, who needs the term socialism—except that it's a handy phrase."

"We believe in industrial democracy," they say. "We believe in civil rights, in international good will and peace, and so on."

But actually, there are other aspects to the socialist movement. The socialist movement, at least in its highest aspirations, was international-minded. It believed that people were people and that they should not be hating one another. And this goes domestically, and this goes internationally.

And on *that* score, I haven't changed. That's what I was and I am. And that's it. That's the evolution of one animal.

Other leaders emphasize the need to preserve private incentive as a reason for their change in thinking:

In the old days, when I was a youngster, we used to stand on soapboxes and say, "What's the remedy for the coal mining industry? Nationalization! What's the remedy for the railroads? Nationalization! The remedy for the whole of industry? Nationalization!"

And we sort of saw a socialist government being voted in and immediately taking over the whole of industry and running it for use instead of for profit.

Now, nobody sees that as a practical thing, even for a socialist government. Even in the countries where you have complete communist control and takeover, they found it necessary, as it were, to denationalize and put back private interests and incentive in certain sections.

Experience has taught us that you cannot take over industry completely and nationalize it. Certain services will cry out for nationalization and be ready for it. Certain services, if you value the health and education of your community, must be carried out almost regardless of cost.

Other sections of industry, if they prove responsive and responsible —there is no reason why they should not be able to continue.

The intangible ideals remain however:

But the values which the socialist movement stood for: the elevation of the human being, the respect for human integrity, the looking toward healthy, happy human beings as the end product of the system —that would be the surviving value that socialism, in my judgment, has.

The respondents who now view socialism as simply an extension of current welfare state measures argue that the whole is equal to the sum of its parts:

Socialists today don't like to talk about public ownership. They prefer to talk about democratic control of the bases of society, and so on.

So socialism today is quite different from what it was at the time I entered the Party in the 1930s—and it was certainly different when I entered from the time of the early founders.

Look, we already have tremendous controls over industry. I don't see, in my lifetime, where we're going to get state ownership.

The only way we're going to get it probably is if these industries collapse and fail, and so on. But even there we don't take over industries if they collapse. Take shipping or railroads. We keep subsidizing them.

So we may have evolved our own forms for handling collapsing industries. You keep the private owners there and you subsidize them.

Even in the area of social welfare you have a strange phenomenon in the United States. One thought at one time, you know, in the area of social welfare, that the state would step in and do everything.

Well in that field, where I know a little bit about things that are happening because I'm in it, the state agencies may contract with voluntary agencies. So even in this area, you have a mixed economy, so to speak, of government services and voluntary services. And by the way, the voluntary services are becoming, more and more, government subsidized services.

So you're getting strange new forms. I've never thought of it this way, but in talking to you I'd say we're likely to stumble on something that is quite different from anything that anyone ever anticipated.

I'm not saying it's going to be good. But it's likely to be better than anything we've had in the past.

Certainly the concept that the state is responsible for the welfare of the citizens—once you get that as an established charter for the citizens—that's important.

And if you begin to build social security from the cradle to the grave, then you don't argue about amounts and sums, and so on.

. . .

There is every sign that there will be more and more socialism in America, but it will come through the old political parties.

Even Eisenhower led to the advance of socialism when he was president. He enlarged the welfare state, the scope of it, the foundations of it. Even its declared enemies will advance it.

It's just part of the times. It comes naturally. It's the thing to do. There are so many practical reasons for it. And to go against the trend means to have cumulative troubles. Everyone of these things has been adopted to avoid troubles.

Eventually, it all will amount to the substance of a new system of which the essential aspect will be socialism. If you use words in the sense that they were used a hundred years ago—a hundred years ago, everything of a progressive nature was called socialism.

Now, we have a hundred other names for it. And what name we use is not the crux of the matter.

In their current conceptions of socialism, our respondents sum up their present values, goals, and images of self, man, and society. Gerhard Lenski [6] defines the conservative point of view as consisting of a distrust of human nature, an image of society as a system which effectively meets certain needs, an insistence on consensus, an underestimation of conflict within the society, a tendency to justify privilege, and a belief in the inevitability of inequality.

While our respondents would certainly not categorize themselves as conservative, we find evidence of each of the above attitudes and beliefs, with the exception of the tendency to justify privilege, in the interviews. These are not typical responses, but they occur.

On the distrust of human nature:

On the one hand you have tremendous opportunity in this country; and on the other hand, you're really in a sense almost frozen into today's corporate world.

And politics as a leverage is almost nonexistent. That is, politics exists to do certain things.

We can improve things. We can make certain things immediately better. But to make radical changes—that's difficult to conceive of.

Certainly not in the near future—unless there was a sudden, disastrous turn for the worst. And if *that* happened, I don't think we'd get socialism, or anything like it.

I think we'd get quite the contrary.

There are scary things. For instance, youth unemployment is growing at a tremendous rate. Now, as long as these kids have some money in their pockets and are able to move around and do some of the things they like to do—go to college and mark time, one thing and another like that—then I don't see them as a terrible threat.

They're going to be a pain in the neck because the rate of what the police call malicious mischievousness goes up, you see—because they have idle hands.

And, on the other hand, there's nothing to motivate them into becoming young storm troopers, as you had in pre-Hitler Germany, or as you had, to some slight degree in the United States, in the thirties.

[6] Gerhard Lenski, *Power and Privilege* (New York: McGraw-Hill Book Co., 1966).

But, given a crisis situation, I think they're more apt to be motivated in a totalitarian way. Historically, this seems to be what has happened.

On an image of society as a system which effectively meets certain needs:

I don't know that any real study has been made of this, but I lived in England, after the War, from 1948 to 1950, during the first labour government—the first postwar labour government.

And so, I had a pretty good chance to see the British economy. And I also did some traveling elsewhere in Europe. And I studied these problems in college.

I was in England for two years on a scholarship at Ruskin College, which is a labour college at Oxford University. I took my degree in politics, philosophy, and economics. And a good deal of it was comparative economics—that kind of thing.

I was amazed at the extent to which, even in Britain as late as 1948, '49, and '50, there were certain types of government regulations, which we take for granted in the United States, that didn't exist in England and apparently didn't exist elsewhere in Europe.

It may be true that they aren't strictly speaking socialist types of control, but. . . .

For example, there is the Pure Food and Drug Act that we have in the United States—and have had, ever since Sinclair wrote *The Jungle*. I think it was adopted in 1910 or something like that.

There is no such law in England and apparently—I'm not so sure of my facts here—they didn't have laws of that kind on the continent either.

There was nothing to compare with our National Labor Relations Act; that is to say, no formal government regulations that guarantee workers the right to organize into unions and give them democratic procedures which enable them to form unions.

In other words, right up until this day, even though it may be true that unionism in most European countries (that is, I'm speaking about Western Europe, democratic European countries) is stronger, there are more workers that are unionized in the United States.

If you look at it from the standpoint of socialistic laws, of government regulation of the economy, and government regulation of workers' rights, in England, there is no similar law.

In England, in a factory where, let us say, hypothetically speaking, ninety-nine per cent of the workers are in favor of a union and the employer is determined not to recognize the union, they have no way of gaining recognition unless they go out on strike and actually beat their brains out on the picket line.

In the United States, we have the National Labor Relations Law which guarantees the right of the workers to vote in a poll and then authorize the union to bargain with the employer.

Similarly with the trust-busting types of legislation. Here we get into an area that's controversial—that is, laws that break up monopolistic controls in industry.

Such antimonopoly laws are much weaker in Britain. And here I'm almost certain I'm correct, they are weaker on the continent as well, than they are in the United States.

It may be true that trust-busting, antimonopoly laws are not, strictly speaking, socialist types of government intervention. They're more inspired by liberal economic philosophy than a socialist economic philosophy.

Yet, they do require state intervention in the economy, and in this sense they're socialistic.

On the need for consensus:

What is needed is something we can all believe in—a common purpose. Everything we believed in has fallen apart and nothing has come along to replace it.

That's the strength of the communist countries—a more or less common purpose. However, I wouldn't suggest that we try to achieve a common purpose in the United States the way the communists have done it.

On conflict in the society:

I don't know whether socialism, the way we understood it back in the early years, has any chance in this country.

Now, I don't hold myself as a theoretician, and a philosopher of socialism, much less, although I consider myself a Marxian. But many of the theories that Marx advocated and advanced now seem to be put into limbo.

Now, one of the main tenets of Marxian socialism is the class struggle—the theory that there is an everlasting struggle going on between those who control everything and have everything in their power, and those who have nothing and have to work for a living.

What do we find as regards to these theories in practice? Here I rely solely upon my own experience as a trade unionist. And I want to cite for you, if I may, the experience I have had along these lines.

We take, for instance, the conditions of the garment workers in the city of New York, who constitute the largest single industry.

Nominally, one would say that the interest of the employers is diametrically opposed to the interest of the workers—that goes without saying. But is it really so, when you come to analyze it in a *true* light? Is it so?

For instance, we in the garment industry have been obliged, in the many years of our dealing with the employers, to realize that not all that is good for the workers is essentially good for the industry.

Now one would think that we have become industrialists, or have become industry minded. But we have come to realize that when industry does not operate satisfactorily and at a fair profit, the workers are affected by it.

We found, for instance, many times in the course of the last twenty years, especially where the employers have been so hard pressed, that the unions have been obliged to come up with their help.

Now that is diametrically opposed to the theories of Marx. His contention was that there is an everlasting struggle and one or the other must give way, but that is not so. I find it quite the reverse in industry.

And on the inevitability of inequality:

Our goal is one of a humane society—a goal of as close to a classless society as possible.

But we do not expect to ever have either a classless society or a complete democracy. We recognize that people have different capabilities and that you cannot have people sufficiently concerned to have democracy fully effective.

What we say is that we must get as close to these things as humanly possible, and that's the most we'll ever be able to do—which means eternal vigilance, for one thing.

The blurring of meanings in contemporary society extends not only to the definition of socialism but to the definition of socialists.

The distinction between radical and conservative, when viewed in substantive terms, is no longer as simple and unequivocal as it once was.

THE FUTURE OF
SOCIALISM IN AMERICA

On the question of the future of socialism in this country, the beliefs of our respondents are complex and, in many cases, ambivalent:

Well, how I feel is this. Oh, I don't know—eventually, *who knows?*

But what I feel is really happening is that we have achieved, in the United States, a level of welfare, a level of economic welfare in our society which is so beyond that of the rest of the world that it isn't reasonable to think in terms of, in the short run, any significant decline of private ownership of industry.

On the other hand, I must say that, if we survive the trends of the world, with *peace*, it seems to me that the survival will be in a world where one or another type of collective ownership will be the more generally accepted form of industrial ownership in the countries of the world.

. . .

I don't think socialism is inevitable. I think it's very desirable. Unfortunately, at this point I agree with Norman Thomas that if we were just betting, the odds are that we would have catastrophe winning out in the world.

The point is that you can't have socialism without people and if we destroy civilization, which is still pretty likely, all talk about socialism becomes meaningless.

But if we don't do that, if we learn to live with each other—even with a balance of terror—long enough to start becoming rational, then it seems to me that the only approach that people will be able to get will be *inevitably* toward a socialist society.

With the kind of automated world we're moving into, there are possibilities of production for a decent life for everybody.

I don't know if we're moving fast enough—I doubt it—but we are moving in that direction, and I see a lot of hopeful signs which would make a socialist approach (and I'm not even concerned anymore whether it's called socialism particularly, although I like it myself) the predominant one.

The atomic era, as I pointed out in the Introduction, makes the retention of long-range goals and the willingness to make long-range predictions extremely difficult and, perhaps, largely a matter of personal optimism or pessimism.

Two leaders who feel that socialism in the form of government ownership of basic industries is inevitable argue that attempts to regulate without ownership would be ineffective:

More members of the socialist movement are now saying that they are for a mixed society where the principal or basic industries are publicly owned and democratically managed and where there is a large place for the cooperative movement.

Also, there would be place in the small industries—in agriculture, in small stores, and so forth—for private enterprise, with the public passing regulatory legislation to correct abuses and protect workers.

And I think this will come.

I think, in the first place, the program to abolish poverty is sort of a frontier program. It doesn't go by any means as far as it should go if they are going to abolish poverty.

I think the advantage is that it's giving the American people a feeling that it is the *duty* of the people, generally, to fight for the abolition of poverty, and once you sort of establish that principle, they are likely to go further.

I think they are going to fumble a great deal, and they are going to try a lot of experiments which will be helpful, to some extent, but which will not eliminate the five million poor, the hard core of unemployment.

And one step which has proved inadequate will lead to another step.

I think what you are likely to get first is an attempt to regulate basic industries, and then, when that regulation is inadequate, there is more of a chance of the public coming in on the various basic industries.

Formerly it was said that if we had public ownership it would be an immense job. Well, we are finding that electronics and computing machines and everything of that sort make it far easier to operate a large corporation, a large public corporation, than in the past.

More and more, we are thinking in terms of public corporations of the type of the TVA which gives the government control of the large ventures, but which allows a great deal of flexibility, as far as the day-to-day activities are concerned.

And every corporation would be conducted somewhat like a private corporation—but for service, not for profit.

All other leaders who believe that socialism, however they may presently define it, is inevitable also argue that it is the only logical outcome of the needs and trends in contemporary, complex, industrial societies:

I'm still optimistic about the possibility that socialism, not in any invidious Birchite sense but as an extension of rational social planning for the society as a whole, will come.

Well, let me put it this way. It seems to me inevitably, well, the word "inevitably" is too strong—but there *are* certain structural pressures which, in any large scale modern society, move toward more effective social planning.

The kinds of interdependence and effects which are generated by change in one area—you have to learn to control and plan for, anticipate, offset, whether you want them or not.

Every modern society moves in that direction. You may call it indicative planning. You may call it indirect planning, the way the British do.

There's a tendency, it seems to me, which has a certain momentum and impetus for the extension of rational planning. Any government is increasingly involved in it.

It comes out of one very simple fact. It comes out of the fact that every society, for all sorts of obvious historical reasons, is now future-oriented—which means that you now try to direct social change. You try to anticipate the nature of social change.

If you're future-oriented, essentially that means an extension of rational planning mechanisms and rational tools. You can't live without them.

Very few leaders believe that a third party, which would replace the Socialist Party but which would have socialist goals, will emerge in a crisis situation. They are all older leaders:

As for the future, I am naturally an optimist. In my opinion, some movement will arise again which will challenge the present-day sloganizers and theoreticians as political agents who are not worthy of our age, and which will expose the slogans such as "the war against poverty" and "the great society" as empty, meaningless panaceas.

What form will it take? When?

There will probably be a rebirth of a third party—maybe enough idealism may be generated again within the trade union movement.

We won't be the agents. We pioneers are too old.

And as for what the party will be called, names don't matter—socialist, etc., etc.

Education and proper understanding of the issues and problems that we face is the most important task that a new party could perform.

Names, labels, are confusing. Capitalism today is a very much modified system, and socialism today is a very much muddled and varied program.

The vast majority of the leaders do not see the possibility of the emergence of a third party in this country. They argue that the Democratic Party is sufficiently oriented toward reform to preclude this possibility:

I would be surprised if a Socialist Party as we knew it would be revived or would have any more success than it has had.

There was a time when I felt, or at least advocated—I don't know how seriously I really felt it—that we could be successful.

I felt that we could reproduce or try to reproduce some sort of a broad British Labour type party in the United States which would constitute, of course, the trade unions and the intellectuals, and the cooperatives, and everybody who would join in the common cause.

I don't see that in the offing any more—much as I would like to.

I think that the existing parties have shown a certain amount of pliability, and they themselves are such broad groupings and subject to internal and external pressures so that they tend to accept criticism and evolve it and assimilate it.

Philip Selznick,[7] in his study of the TVA, utilized the concept of co-optation to refer to the process of absorption of new and

[7] Philip Selznick, *T.V.A. and the Grass Roots* (Berkeley, California: University of California Press, 1949), p. 13.

possible hostile elements into the leadership or policy-making structure of organizations. This technique is used by established leadership as a means to avert threats to its stability or existence. Co-optation has been the fate of innumerable political dissenters in this country, particularly since the 1930s.

A high value is placed on innovation and nonconformity in our society, especially by the upper stata. Innovators, as long as they are not destructive and do not threaten basic interests or basic institutional change, are highly regarded and even imitated.

The process of industrialization involves the replacement of hand-fashioned, noninterchangeable tools by standardized machines with standardized parts, which produce standardized goods. We have, in other words, mass production and its corollary, mass consumption. To operate this kind of economy, standardized skills and education are required. The question then becomes, "Do we have, or are we getting, standardized people?" A controversy has raged and still rages among social scientists and other intellectuals, over the answer.[8]

Proponents of increasing differentiation in our society argue that the division of labor and differences in age, race, education, religion, and ethnicity mitigate the homogenizing effects of mass education and of the mass media.

Whatever the facts, originality is highly valued in our society, and artistic and political innovators have been experiencing unprecedented efforts at co-optation in recent years:

> There are complaints among intellectuals that the moment they have a new idea, a new concept, it's immediately grabbed up by the mass media and becomes diffused.

> You simply can't distinguish yourself by being offbeat any more. *Life* magazine immediately puts your picture into a feature story, and you are already part of the establishment before you can decide that you are not.

[8] See, Daniel Bell, *The End of Ideology* (New York: The Free Press, 1962), Chapter I; also, Bernard Rosenberg and David Manning White, eds., *Mass Culture* (Glencoe, Illinois: The Free Press, 1957), particularly the introductory essays by the editors.

Bernard Rosenberg and Norris Fliegel, in their study *The Vanguard Artist,* observed that a similar difficulty is experienced by successful artists in contemporary society. The problem has shifted from "How to remain separate without being cut off" from the rest of the society to "How to remain separate" from the rest of society.[9] Co-optation is the trend for artistic as well as political innovators.

The fact of co-optation by a reform-oriented government is regarded by some leaders as an additional factor which makes the emergence of a third party in this country highly unlikely. And no leader, in any generation, believes that the Socialist Party will ever achieve power in this country, directly, and in its identity as the Socialist Party of America.

ON REALIGNMENT

Whatever the economic, political, and social goals to which the leaders presently adhere, on the question of means for achieving these goals there is pretty general agreement that efforts should be directed toward influencing the Democratic Party in a more reformist direction. Individuals who are members of the Socialist Party and who maintain this position, where it is called the realignment position, define the present role of the Socialist Party as an educational institution. They regard participation of Socialist Party members in the political activities of the Democratic Party, or other organizations interested in economic reform, as legitimate, desirable, and appropriate.

The majority, in all generations, believes that this is the only realistic alternative or politically effective course which is open to socialists at the present time:

As you may know, I'm a strong supporter of the realignment theory. I think the Socialist Party will never become, I'll make this a flat statement—this Party that I'm a member of will never become a serious electoral factor in the United States.

[9] Bernard Rosenberg and Norris Fliegel, *The Vanguard Artist* (Chicago: Quadrangle Books, 1965), p. 150.

This is because of its reputation as a failure, if for no other reason. This has already been thoroughly established. It's quite generally accepted that the Socialist Party is not going to be the vehicle for a new third party or new feeling for a third party movement in the United States.

If there were such a feeling for a third party movement, it would be for a *new* party. People don't like to start out with an instrument that already has deeply ingrained upon the public the notion that it is a failure. The Party is regarded as a "has-been."

I personally suspect that political progress is not going to take the form of a third party in the United States. As far as I can see, there have been situations in which the possibilities of a third party development were much better than they have ever been in my lifetime. And it never worked in the past.

I think the Democratic Party now is firmly established as the party of the underdog in the United States, that all the progressive elements in the country are identified with the Democratic Party—that is, the organized working class in the trade union movement, the majority of the Negro population, the majority of the Jewish population, and the liberal intellectuals.

They regard the Democratic Party as *their* party. And I think if they shift to the left in their own thinking that they'll translate this shift into political terms inside the Democratic Party.

So, the American equivalent of the mass socialist labor movement of Europe, if it's ever to take place—and I think it may—I suspect will take place inside the Democratic Party, and *not* as a result of the socialists surreptitiously boring from within.

That is a very distorted and vulgar notion that some socialists, who are against the whole realignment theory and who are loyal to the old traditional independent electoral notion, have.

That's sheer idiocy—aside from the fact that it's the conception of political work that I reject, on principle.

I'm for proclaiming our identity as socialists openly. I'm for our getting in there. When a socialist is in a union, I'm for his working with his COPE* organization, as many of them have, to get into ward and precinct Democratic Party organizations—and not only as socialist unionists, but as socialists.

* Committee on Political Education, political arm of the AFL-CIO.

In California, for example, I'm for socialists joining and being active in the Democratic Party clubs and, in New York, in the reform movement.

And I think there will be similar movements that will develop in the future. I'm for being active in these movements—openly, expressing our ideas, trying to convince people of our ideas.

I'm for retaining the Socialist Party, by the way, as an educational instrument and as an organization that can publish material, that can conduct educational conferences, that can be a place where people can develop new ideas and have a means of putting them forward, and as an instrument for retaining contact with the international socialist movement, the Socialist International.

It has many uses, but *not* as a political party aiming to gain power because that's a will-o'-the-wisp. It's not going to happen. I think that kind of work has to be done in the Democratic Party.

I'm not a prophet. It may be that I'm wrong. Maybe something will happen along the line that will disillusion vast, vast numbers of people who are now loyal to the Democratic Party and make them think in third party terms.

If so, it's okay with me. I'm not a Democrat basically, and I have no stake in the Democratic Party.

It's simply that I think political realism dictates that this is the area now and so far as I can see, for the foreseeable future, in which effective political work can be done.

While the majority of the leaders accept the realignment position, those who are still members of the Party evidence differences on this issue along generational lines. The oldest generation is most apt to be opposed to the realignment positions. This reflects the generational differences on this issue that exist within the entire Party at the present time. The identity as a socialist is too firmly entrenched for many members of the World War I Generation who are still members of the Party, and the feeling of distinctness and separateness politically precludes the possibility of activity within the Democratic Party:

Some socialists are working in the ADA* or in the labor movement

* Americans for Democratic Action

or working within the Democratic Party with the idea that they will be a sort of educational nucleus within that broader movement to turn it in the farmer, labor, liberal direction and to get rid of the Southern reactionaries.

I can't do that, as I have never been able to feel that the Democratic Party *can* be made that instrument. I still feel, I think fundamentally, that there has to be a new movement eventually, a new party, which will displace probably the Republican Party and become part of the two party system.

But, I'm not dogmatic about it. I am not saying that I am right and the others are wrong. That's all they *can* do at present.

Primarily, I couldn't do it because I feel it wouldn't work. The Democratic Party and the administration stand for so many things that I don't believe in, that I don't think I could *stomach* it.

I just don't think I could work in it. That's all.

This is a current issue over which factions divide in the Socialist Party:

This is a little unfair maybe, but this is what I think. It isn't so much that they are interested in changing the Democratic Party as that they want to get close to the power sources of the Democratic Party.

And they subordinate foreign policy to their grand program. The domestic scene starts to take precedence over everything else. For example, on Cuba some of the realignment group were in favor of invading Cuba. "Castro is a totalitarian, after all—a communist," they said.

Now, I wouldn't have found that so terrible except that after a while what happens, of course, is that people start thinking of you, their so-called comrade, as being the worst person in the world.

They start looking inward and never looking outward. After a while you get a tremendous feeling of "What is this charnel house we're in?"

You know, the Socialist Party seems less and less meaningful. The socialist alternative is less and less meaningful. The labor party concept becomes more meaningful or something else becomes more meaningful.

Besides, there's a certain question of honesty. I don't really know if

it's possible for somebody to stand up in the Democratic Party and
say, "Nominate me for office."

I've been a member of the Reform Democratic clubs and so on. I'm
not essentially opposed to that sort of activity.

But it's a matter of elections among other things, you know—not
just a series of clubs where people pass resolutions. The resolutions
aren't meaningful unless they're carried out by legislative representatives.

So I don't know if you can really expect, in too many years in the
United States, under the situations in the world, for people to get up
and say, "Nominate me to be your state senator. I'm a socialist you
see. That's what I am. I'm a socialist."

I'm thirty-two. If I were ten years older I might do it—ten years
more of disappointments, ten years more disillusioned, then I might
very well think about doing that. If I were five years younger, I'd join
the New Left. But I'm not quite that. You see, I'll tell you. It's all in
how you conceive of yourself, right?

I used to think of myself as an organizer, eager, etc., etc. I don't
think of myself as that anymore. I'm a teacher who's interested in
ideas, and I'm going to pursue some of the ideas. That's all it amounts
to. I leave it to the organizers. Everybody has his function—let the organizers organize.

Ten years from now, maybe it will be a different thing. Five years
ago, it was a different thing.

The top leadership of the Party at present supports the realignment position, although they do not personally and actively participate in Democratic Party activities.

One of these leaders, no longer active but still a member of the
Party and a strong supporter of the realignment position, gives
his view of why socialism will come through the established
parties:

You take a radical—communist, socialist, Trotskyist—it doesn't matter. He has been in his organization for five years, ten, fifteen, twenty,
thirty years.

He has given all his time, all his thoughts, and all his activity to it.
He's worked for it, some harder—some less actively, but he's worked
for it. That has been his political life.

It has also been his social life: all his social activities were concentrated in or around that political organization. It's been his personal life to a very great extent—all his friends, or virtually all, are his Party comrades.

That is the general tendency of everybody in the radical political movement—it is a world of its own, as it were.

Some are completely absorbed in this world. But even the least active and the least dedicated are, to a great extent, involved in this world. It is their activity, their hope, their aspiration, the embodiment of their ideals—it is their world.

Then some critical situation develops which shatters this world for you, for *you* as an active person, for *you* who've spent so much time—I mean in the sense of adherence to—so many years, who had so much confidence, so much belief in it.

And that structure collapses around you, not because of this or that little difference of opinion, but something more basic than that, something comparable, say, to the developments in the Communist Party at the time of Khrushchev's revelations and the Hungarian events.

It was *shattering* for some of them, shattering. "So much of what we believed," they might say to themselves, "has proved to be false, spurious."

What is commonly called the disenchantment, sets in. You are now thirty, forty, perhaps fifty, in some cases sixty, and you are faced with the problem, "I can no longer continue in this."

This is especially true in the communist movement, because there a difference of opinion cannot last more than a minute or two, so to speak. You either fall into line, or you are *out*.

Then comes your problem. WHAT DO I DO NOW? Well, most people in such situations are burned out.

Not less than tens of thousands of former communists, tens of thousands, maybe more, and tens of thousands of socialists, for one reason or another that would come under the rubric of political disenchantment, have dropped out of political life altogether, certainly have dropped out of a political organization.

They found that they had been wrong or that they had been futile—not wrong, but futile. They still cling to their ideas, but the organization that embodied these ideas, for one reason or another, could not realize them.

It's all right for a kid to be in an organization for a week or a month, or a year or two, and then jump into another. His whole life is still ahead of him.

But the older radical who feels disillusioned—his life is shot to hell; he can't start a new one. He can't start on *anything*.

So I don't believe in the possibilities of a resurgence of the socialist movement in the United States on the basis of the old radical generation, no.

Individuals, here and there, absolutely incredible and exceptional individuals like Thomas, can still keep going, twenty-four hours a day, seven days a week. But how many are there like that? One, two, twelve, fifteen? It's nothing. It's wonderful by my standards, but it's not a movement. Those are just magnificent socialist individuals. But it's not a movement. It's a sect.

But I feel that social forces, political forces, groupings in the country that the radical movement in the past either ignored or did not assess properly—did not give the proper weight to—are developing in their own way with a *minimum* of the old socialist and communist influences among them, toward what I believe will emerge eventually, I do not know when, as an American socialist movement.

I don't know what it will be called. And, of course, it doesn't matter what it's called. I would like to have it called socialism for traditional reasons—because I like political consistency. . . .

Socialism in this country will come gradually—not tomorrow, but the day after.

And it will come, *not* as a gradual accretion of Socialist Party recruits—one, or two, or five, or five hundred—but as a force, a yeast inside existing political organizations, not as a rival but as a partner— as in England where the Labour Party eventually adopted socialist programs.

Socialists must work within these structures as socialists, maintaining their identity as socialists and as an integral part of the system— not something alien, outside the structure, but as individuals who are operating within the system and who are *conscious* of the direction of political and social evolution.

Socialists in the reform movement of the Democratic Party are accepted as socialists and *respected* in their socialist identity.

And I think socialism will come *above all* in the economically advanced countries, because they have the wealth. If there is plenty, sharing and redistributing is not a problem.

If there are seven pairs of shoes and ten people who need shoes, you will have conflict. But, if there are seventy pairs of shoes—then *everybody* can have a pair of shoes.

On the question of the tendency of people to take on the values and attitudes of those with whom they associate and the possible loss, therefore, to the Party, of members who work actively within the Democratic Party:

Of course, there's the possibility of the dilution of the socialism. I've seen it a million times. I've seen socialists go into trade unions. They begin to negotiate with the employers. Some of them begin to modify their position, to modify their values or become antagonistic to those values. That's the trouble with politics. I've seen it a million times.

And that's the advantage of, and what encourages, a sect. Since a sect does not have to deal with these things except in theory, it can retain its uncompromising position, and that's very attractive to idealistic people. It is to me.

But just as if I go into a trade union I can lose some of my values and perhaps abandon them, if I am that certain kind of guy, and if that is the negative aspect of that kind of work for socialists, I must also bear in mind that there is a positive aspect for a different kind of guy.

If I stick to my views, I also have the opportunity which the life of a sect does not afford me, of influencing non-socialists in a socialist direction.

There is a push and a pull. The non-socialist, the mood, the element, the environment, tend to weaken my socialism, I grant that.

But at the same time, is there not also a pull on my side? Can't I, by demonstrating what a socialist can do in the trade union and economic field, also demonstrate that socialism cannot be so terribly bad?

I can talk to the non-socialist. I don't appear to him as an outsider advocating this, that, and the other thing. I appear to him as a friend, as a comrade, as a fellow-worker, participating in his life on an equal basis. Why can't I move him toward socialism?

It's been done in Europe; it's been done in absolutely genuinely

Anglo-Saxon non-European countries like Canada, New Zealand, and Australia.

There is no innate quality about the United States that prohibits me from succeeding here.

Another argument which is given for the realignment position is the disadvantage of the socialist label:

Personally, I started to give up the idea that we should be a separate electoral party very early. I remember I called a meeting of a few top leaders in 1942, in New Jersey, where we were living at the time.

I said, "Look, I'm going to show you the evidence. There are many examples to prove that socialist ideas can often be promoted openly by people who are politically involved in the Democratic and Republican Parties."

We had actually a couple of very cute cases. I can't even remember them any more, but there had been two people, one a Democrat and one a Republican, elected to the state legislatures in, I think, two New England states. One was certainly New England.

They had openly campaigned on socialist platforms during the depression, in the early Roosevelt period, and had been elected by the voters.

I said, "Look, isn't this the best evidence you can have that just by changing the label—without not only not changing the content, but not even changing the language of what they were advocating—they were able to get the support of voters who wouldn't have voted for them under the socialist label, simply because the traditional holds are so powerful?"

But no one would go along with me—no one at all.

Not only the fact of the willingness of the Democratic Party to institute reform, but also the ease with which reform is accomplished, with the current concentration of power in the executive branch of government, is given as an argument for working within the established parties:

Changes have taken place within our—I often even hesitate to call it capitalist society today—within our established society that we would have said many years ago would be absolutely unanticipated.

I wouldn't say impossible—but unanticipated, incredible. And cer-

tainly that the sources of these changes would lie in presidenti
actions—Johnson, or the last one, Kennedy. . . .

In our minds, years ago, these *couldn't* be the source of tremendou
social change, except as grudging concessions to an overwhelmir
mass. And today we just know that this isn't so.

Johnson, for whom I have no personal regard whatsoever—no sp
cial antagonism, but no regard, I mean I don't think he's a man
high idealism or great depth of understanding or anything of th
sort—he can just flip off, in the manner of an incidental interview,
kind of major social change that we might have put years into stru
gling for.

ON MAJOR SOCIAL PROBLEMS

Not only does the World War I Generation retain the tradition
definition of socialism and the belief in the inevitability of socia
ism to a greater extent than the younger generations, but the
also demonstrate a greater retention of the original internation
orientation.

The World War I Generation is more concerned about war an
the problems of international relations than the younger genera
tions. A large majority of the leaders in this generation who di
cussed this question feel that the possibility of war is the greate
single problem in America today. Unemployment is the next mo
frequently mentioned problem; civil rights, as a major problem,
not mentioned at all.

In contrast, the younger generations are more concerned wit
domestic problems, relatively: automation, particularly, an
poverty and civil rights.

One Interwar Generation leader believes that the tradition
international orientation of the movement has been damaging t
its growth:

Aside from the question of socialism as an economic philosoph
the Socialist Party is also involved in the whole problem of intern
tional relations.

The socialist movement has tended to be a pacifist movement, c

e theory that war is the product of the capitalist class. And today the
cialist movement is still very much influenced by a pacifist strain.

In my early religious years, I was a pacifist. Today, I believe that
cifism has nothing to offer to a solution of international problems,
d, therefore, I find myself increasingly at odds with positions that a
ajority of socialists would take.

For instance, I'm not ready for the United States to pull out of
etnam. I don't know enough about the Santo Domingo thing. I
uld tend to take the traditional socialist position about what the
ministration did there.

Pacifism has been another one of the issues that has proved damag-
g to the growth of the socialist movement. It has really been two
parate movements in one. And you can believe in the economic
ogram and not believe in the second body of doctrine relating to the
nduct of international affairs.

This had tended to cause splits in the socialist movement. People
ho should have been united on domestic issues would split the Party
cause of the international questions. You fritter away the support
r the basic idea, the *economic* idea of socialism.

The effort to make socialism an all-inclusive concept—one that
plies to all of the social problems of our time—has weakened,
erefore, the attempt to deal with economic problems.

ationalism and a domestic orientation are more prominent in
e perspectives of the younger generations.

ON THE NEW LEFT

the Introduction, I pointed out that the Old Left and the New
eft in this country are divided on the question of means and on
e question of ends. The New Left has emphasized short-range
als: better jobs, housing, and education; and the principle of
rect action: greater participation in local community decision-
aking processes by the poor. They have sought to organize the
nemployed and the nonunionized masses in the rural South and
e ghetto North. The new generation of radicals views the Old
eft as rigid, doctrinaire, and, above all, ineffectual.

The Old Left, at least those representatives in our study who discussed this topic, have a variety of feelings about the New Left. One leader expresses a combination of indignation and sadness about the new radicals:

I think we're irrelevant to the New Left. You know, we're good people—Norman Thomas went down to Mississippi and spoke a few dozen times. A guy like Jack Newfield, who's a socialist, is regarded as a good man; Mike Harrington is respected.

But, like many times in our history the influence or individuals connected with the socialist movement is greater than the influence of the movement as a whole.

Even the YPSLs have been drifting away. Many of them have joined the New Left. I attended their last convention in Chicago as a representative of the Socialist Party. This was in 1965, I guess.

It had just been taken over by a very small and *not* radical group. I say, "not radical" really very advisedly. The leader of this group's caucus, a fellow named Bob, got up to make a speech and he said, "Listen," he said, "we don't know anything. As a matter of fact, if you face reality, we don't know anything about anything at all. We don't understand how capitalism really works. But," he said, "we do know this. We know that the social democratic, communist, Trotskyist, and syndicalist points of view are failures."

At the convention, there was a guy sitting at the back of the room —this is a *YPSL* convention—who, if you had to paint a picture of the quintessence of what the *Saturday Evening Post* small-town Ohio housewife thinks about the radical movement, this guy would have looked like it.

First of all, his hair was combed in the center of his forehead, like Bakunin, coming down on either side, down to about his ear lobes.

He was wearing a red bandana kerchief around his neck. He had on a Levi work jacket. Well, that wasn't too bad. But dangling around his neck, and right in the middle of his chest (I swear, in the middle of his chest), he had a *salami!*

And from time to time, during the convention, this incredible creep would take out his imitation eighteenth-century knife and slice off a piece of the salami—chopping away at it, you know, and nodding pensively all the while.

The thing about it that was interesting was that he was obviously not to be taken seriously and these people didn't take him seriously, but they tolerated him at the same time.

It wasn't a question of acceptance—of accepting somebody with distinct mannerisms, and so forth. It was a question of the entire tone of the convention being that since they didn't take themselves seriously why should they take *him* seriously? "As crazy as we are," they were saying, "why should we object to this nut?"

So what happened is that this one faction took over. And they were so incredible. For example, Norman Thomas' birthday was coming up, and a motion came up to wish Norman Thomas a happy birthday —an actual, formal kind of motion!

But one-third of the convention voted against wishing him a happy birthday! Why? Who knows? Because Norman Thomas is old and they were young. Norman Thomas is from New York and they were mostly from Chicago. Who knows?

Because—did you see *What's New Pussycat?* Do you remember the psychoanalytic group session thing where everybody kept hanging around doing strange things? Well, that was the atmosphere of this particular convention.

Nobody cared. These were people who agreed among themselves to do something. They were going to take over, you see. And they didn't care. I mean they didn't take anything seriously. They were just going through the motions, you see.

Generally, the leaders tend to identify with and to feel sympathetic toward the serious and deeply committed members of the latest generation of radicals. Disapproval centers on what is defined as the nihilism, or the confusion and lack of long-range goals of the New Left:

I am very sympathetic with what we are now calling the New Left. I know why they hate so much of the present establishment, and so much of the present bourgeois life, and all the rest of it.

I can understand why some of them even think they hate America. In contrast with our ideals, we've done pretty badly.

But I wish they had a more definite answer. It's a kind of nihilist objection that they raise, rather than an adequate solution for a world where you've got to accept the fact that we are closely tied together, that you can't revert to small, anarchist cooperative colonies and keep life going.

. . .

The New Left is very dramatic, has been very dramatic. A few years ago, I sat in on a session of young New Left people, all of them upper age bracket college students, one of them being a graduate student.

Their parents, their families, were all essentially liberals and so-cialists. There were five students. Two came from socialist back-grounds; three from liberal backgrounds.

These students were asked to speak to an audience of their elders, their parents and people of their parents' age group, and their grand-parents' age group, about what was happening on the campus—this new stir of movement and thought.

All of them agreed that the students rejected ideology. They were not interested in an all-encompassing analysis and approach to the society. This pragmatic approach they said, was based on the fact of the bomb and nuclear warfare. Life could be very short and, therefore, long-range plans were not warranted.

I have a feeling that it wasn't the bomb that bothered them, but some feeling of insecurity that led them to bury themselves in the immediate problems where they can achieve some sense of results and positive achievement.

I don't know what those five would say today. I think some of them now speak differently.

I think that the New Left on campus is going to go through a period of change. I'd like to see what happens after the Vietnam problem is put on the shelf, assuming that it doesn't result in an age of warfare.

I would hope that they will show a greater concern with our general problems—problems that must be faced by the nation as well as by college students.

These are not as dramatic in character as a war or as immediate as the fight for the rights of Negroes—one-ninth of the population of the country. These are dramatic missions which draw on emotional sup-port.

And the question of urban planning, the question of social planning for control of our economy so that the needs of all people will be met—these are dry subjects.

I don't know. I'm hoping, since I think this is going to be the major problem of the next twenty-five years, I'm hoping that there will be this concern on their part.

. . .

There's an element of utopianism in the ideas of the New Left, just as there was in my own ideas when I first became a socialist. The problem is that they lack, as I did, a basic sense of political realism, which, I suppose, comes from experience and maturity.

. . .

I think the most moral people in the United States now are the New Left. But I think this group is somewhat confused in their conception of what morality is.

They believe that you can separate political morality from individual morality, in the sense that taking a stand on civil rights, and so forth, they see as being separate from and different from the kinds of personal relationships that they have with people.

They are sympathetic to pot, and LSD, and one thing and another. There's something about having an orientation to experimentation upon oneself, you know, using one's body as an experimental mechanism for a chemical, that I find very upsetting.

Our respondents do not believe that the poor can form the potential mass base for a radical movement:

The students are making their base in the unemployed, which is the wrong base. The unemployed don't move anything. When the poor and unemployed and Negroes all account for only about a fourth or, at best, a third of our population, you don't have the motive force, really, that you had back in the 1930s when the poor and the Negroes and the unemployed accounted for about two-thirds of the population.

The alternative, if I were thinking out loud, or dreaming in terms of looking for a motive force, would be the fact that we have got leisure time, and our people have been to college now.

And the middle class has acquired enough material goods to be satiated. Now it can always go out and acquire more. That's not the issue. You can create wants indefinitely.

But there is a certain point after which the creation of material wants becomes less meaningful, or the acquisition of material products becomes less meaningful than the acquisition of psychic values.

This is not true of a working-class person for whom it is very, very important that they have medical treatment and a home. And they do not have time to be sentimental.

They don't have time to be sentimental about a pet dog. If the pet dog is sick, the pet dog will die. If the pet cat is sick, the pet cat will be drowned. They don't have time. They have *very real* problems of food, medicine, and illness.

Now the middle class is sentimental. They have time for it. And, I think, with a college education they may have time to stop worrying about acquiring more and more, and worry more about the nature of society.

In this sense you may have what you have never before had in history—that is, a motive force which is no longer the poor, but the wealthy.

They might revolutionize society after they have acquired all that they need.

The leaders do not have much hope that the New Left movement will affect the course of political events in this country:

You have to remember that nothing is more transitory than the college generation. By definition they disappear, so that in four years you have a whole new group. And there isn't very much carry-over.

They may develop in some entirely new direction. It's good to see this development, and it's good to talk to these kids even if you disagree with them on one or another point—about Maoism, or whatever they seem to be activated by.

But you don't build a movement, or a movement doesn't get built, by something which is by definition, transitory—college generations.

. . .

I feel the differences between the Old Left and the New Left are inevitable—without taking it too seriously.

I guess I used to feel this way about the Militants and the Old Guard. I used to feel the difference between them is not revolution versus evolution, but twenty years in their age levels.

And this is pretty much true now. Now SDS * is the big thing. About four years ago, when it was first coming up and the LID** was very unhappy about some of the things they heard, I took on the

* Students for a Democratic Society
** League for Industrial Democracy, a reform-oriented educational organization originally socialist in perspective.

chairmanship of the Student Activities Committee of the LID, and I went off to a two-day conference with a group of SDS kids.

I led a discussion and then just participated. I had to report back to the LID, and I said, "Look, the new revolutionary ideas—I listened and listened, but I didn't hear any new revolutionary ideas." That's really true.

I don't say I agreed with all the ideas. That's a different thing. But I'd heard them all twenty years ago. There was nothing there, really, that was different.

And this we've had to learn simply because we're parents. The young people have to *feel* that these ideas are new and represent rejection of the old.

And I think if some of us who are older would be mature enough to say, "Okay, so they reject us, and their ideas are new, and everything we did was wrong. Let's start by accepting that, and then let's see what they're talking about. If we talk about the ideas themselves, we'll be much further ahead."

Now I happen to disagree with a lot of their attitudes on the irrelevancy of communist identity. But I must say they're not new either. They say, "Don't tell me if someone is a communist or not; tell me if he's joining my fight."

Well, that's the same thing really, just a slight variation in verbiage, on what was said so many times during the popular front. And I'm not talking about the people who were being deceptive.

It meant just that. They *really* meant, "I'm against fascism. Don't tell me whether somebody's a communist or a socialist or a liberal. Tell me if he's against fascism."

That's just what they meant. They didn't mean anything else. And that's just what these kids mean.

I think that these kids, and very rapidly, will go through the same set of experiences, with slight variations, and will end up with the same disillusionments and divisions.

Some of them will end up here. Some of them will end up there. And most of them will end up in good jobs in corporations.

CONCLUSION

In the preceding chapters we have seen that the experience of being a socialist and a leader of the Socialist Party in this country has encompassed much more than can be conveyed by a description of the public statements and actions of the people who were interviewed. For many, socialism was and, to some extent, still is a central core of identity which persists regardless of present political goals and current political affiliations.

The system of values and beliefs embodied in socialist ideals has been a unifying and integrating force, particularly in the lives of the older leaders, determining not only intellectual and political orientations but friendships, occupational and marital choices, and leisure and recreational activities.

They were attracted to the movement on the basis of previous socialization in home or neighborhood, or as a result of a personal and independent search for meaning and purpose, and they were molded by the movement. They all share certain value orientations: a strong intellectual bent, humanism, a highly ethical approach to human relations, and a willingness to give time and energy to social goals. Authoritarianism and totalitarianism, in any of their various forms, are abhorrent to them.

Their ideals have been modified with changing times, but they still entertain visions of a world where human needs, psychic and material, will be better met. They reject the materialism, brutality, and dishonesty in certain aspects of American life, and they tend to emphasize ethical considerations in their present goals, however varied these goals may be.

A variety of circumstances and influences, operating in combination, brought them into the socialist movement: reading, family, neighborhood, and peer group influences, reactions to poverty, exposure to leaders of the Party, and psychological need for commitment, friends, or identity.

Their present conceptions of socialism vary considerably and reflect the difficulty in maintaining fixed and explicit goals, given the increasing complexity and constantly accelerating rate of social change in highly industrialized societies. They tend to emphasize more effective government control and planning of production and distribution, as well as the extension of welfare state reforms.

The failure of the Socialist Party and the socialist movement is viewed as a complex phenomenon not readily explained. The oldest leaders, while they are aware of the failure of the Socialist Party as a political organization, tend to deny the failure of the socialist movement in this country. They point to certain political and economic changes that have occurred in the United States over the past fifty years which they feel derive, in some measure, from the ideas and activities of the socialist movement.

The most frequently mentioned reason for the failure of the Party and the movement in America is the economic reforms instituted by the government, dating from the Progressive era. Other common responses to this question are the factionalism within the Party, its failure to capture the support of the labor movement because of the inapplicability of socialist ideology to the needs and desires of the working class, the ease of social mobility and the weakness of the class struggle in America, as well as the two-party electoral system, ethnic differences which mitigated against the possibility of common action by the working class, and the fact that the socialist ideology was European in origin.

No leader believes that the Socialist Party in its present form will ever achieve power in America; very few believe that a third party will emerge to take its place in a time of crisis. Yet many, particularly in the older and in the youngest generation, continue with their Party activities. The younger leaders do so with the hope of influencing the Democratic Party to enact more far-reaching economic reforms. They regard these efforts as the only realistic alternative open to them at the present time. They retain their socialist goals, but these goals tend to be vague and are quite diverse. The principle of public responsibility for the welfare of all citizens is the major value which survives and underlies their current visions of socialism.

The fact of having been born at a particular time and having come to political maturity during a certain period in history has affected not only the typical life experiences of the leaders but also their characteristic ways of looking at the world. Despite similarities, there are differences between the generations which emerge, sometimes quite dramatically, in the reminiscences.

Self-images are somewhat different: the image of the pragmatist tends to replace the image of the idealist among the younger leaders.

The influences which led to the decision to join the Party were somewhat different: economic factors were far more salient for the World War I Generation; family and neighborhood influences were more decisive for the Interwar Generation; and reading (as an initial stimulus), college peer group influences, and psychological factors were more significant to the World War II Generation.

In the succeeding generations, there has been a progressive loss of idealism and optimism, a progressive loss of an all-embracing ideology, a progressive loss of certainty and community—at least initially, and in the sense that the World War II Generation tended to follow more individual paths into the movement and were more apt to have engaged in a deliberate search for a socialist group.

The progressive loss of certainty, optimism, and idealism is indicated by the fact that the World War I Generation is more apt to have retained the traditional definition of socialism, to believe that socialism is inevitable and not anachronistic, to stress ethical and nontangible humanistic goals in their present conceptions of socialism, and to believe that their decision to become socialists was purely rational.

Expressions of disillusionment are more pervasive and more impassioned in the Interwar Generation than in the other generations. A greater proportion of the leaders in this generation have left the Party; they are most likely to feel that socialism, as traditionally defined, is anachronistic or unnecessary; they are least apt to feel that socialism, however they may presently define it, is inevitable.

Certain attitudes and values of the World War II Generation seem to move in the direction of the New Left: negative attitudes toward communism are less vehement, there is a greater emphasis on pragmatism and short-term political effectiveness, and apocalyptic visions are gone.

The younger leaders of the Socialist Party, like the New Left, do not speak of solidarity, brotherhood, the inherent goodness of man, or the possibility of a classless or conflict-free society. The latest generations of radicals are all responding to the same set of changed social conditions: the atomic era, the increased complexity of social structure, the widespread bureaucratization of social life, the concentration of power at the top of the various institutional hierarchies, and the residue of disillusioning external events and disabusing psychological and social-scientific theories of human behavior and human limitations that have become part of the cultural heritage in America.

The greater acceptance of the realignment position by the younger generations in the Socialist Party may herald its final demise as a separate and distinguishable organization dedicated to political protest and radical social change. Whether or not this will occur, one thing seems clear: generations are ephemeral, but protest abides.

Social movements will continue to arise as long as there are discrepancies in a society between its ideals and the social reality, between its laws and its operational norms, between the values and privileges of those in power and those not in power. In traditional, agricultural societies religious movements appear, advocating other-worldly ends. In modern, industrial societies secular movements emerge, advocating this-worldly ends and the rational means for achieving these ends.

Perhaps, given the conditions of increasing abundance and heightened conflict between the generations in contemporary, automating societies, the mere fact of age and generation will become more significant than economic class or class identifications in determining the recruitment of active political dissenters in the future. The direction of political protest, left or right, may be largely a matter of class identifications and political socialization, but in modern society the fact of active protest seems to be increasingly a matter of age.

The young are better equipped to innovate in all areas of life. They have more freedom and energy; they are less committed to the society as it is. They do not have as much to lose with change, and what they wish to gain economically, for themselves or others, in an automating economy may become less important as time goes on. It is certainly less obvious, even now, in some dissenting groups of affluent social origins. The Hippie social movement, insofar as it rejects materialism and emphasizes expressive, participative behavior (rather than passive, spectator types of recreation) may be a harbinger of the future adaptation of man to an automated economy of staggering material abundance, and to an historically unprecedented amount of leisure time for almost all men.[1]

In their early stages, social movements are usually led by charismatic leaders—leaders who arise in a time of crisis, and who are believed to possess extraordinary or even magical qualities. Charismatic leaders have generally been young, they have

[1] For a discussion of the possible effects of increased abundance and leisure on our society, see Donald N. Michael, *The Next Generation* (New York: Vintage Books, 1965).

not been good family men, and they do not occupy high level institutionalized positions in the societies in which they arise.[2] Adult responsibilities are the great deterrent to radical innovation and radical protest.

The forms that political protest will take in a society—the means, the ends, the justifying ideas, the scope of desired change and the inspiration for change—will vary with the time, the place, and the society.

What continues is the rebirth of new generations—of new human resources and new potential agents of deliberate social change in modern times.

[2] See Max Weber's discussion of charisma and the routinization of charisma in, Max Weber, *The Theory of Social and Economic Organization*, trans. and ed. by A. M. Henderson and Talcott Parsons (Glencoe: The Free Press, 1947), pp. 263–73.

APPENDIX A

METHODS

The interviews took place in 1965 and 1966, over a period of eighteen months. The leaders who were approached initially are quite well known in the socialist movement in this country. They were reached by letter. Additional names of leaders were obtained by asking those whom I had already interviewed to recommend other individuals who have had substantial political or intellectual influence within the Party. All leaders who were eventually interviewed were named by several other leaders, at least. Almost all have worked full-time for the Party and have held high-level positions such as membership on the National Executive Committee. Most of the oldest leaders have run for political office on the Socialist Party ticket in local or national elections.

Leaders, rather than rank and file members of the Party, were selected for interviewing, because it was felt they would be more articulate, more informed about Socialist Party history, and more apt to demonstrate in crystallized form the values and attitudes of members of the Socialist Party in this country.

Leaders of Jewish, Eastern, and Central European origin are over-represented, and leaders of protestant origin underrepresented in the total sample. This is due to the unavailability, because of death, of many of the early leaders of the Party, who were active when the composition of the Party was more varied. For this reason, it cannot be assumed that the findings reported here would be applicable to the total universe of leaders active in the Socialist Party since its beginning.

The purpose of the study was explained in the initial letter: to further understanding of the meaning of the movement to those who were actively involved, and to provide information that is not usually found in historical accounts of the Party. When interviewed, many of the leaders, expressed an enthusiasm for the study and an interest in having it done. This may explain the surprisingly favorable response to the initial letters. Very few leaders refused to be interviewed.

The oldest leaders were interviewed first because of the pressure of possible illness or death. Several leaders, in fact, have died since the completion of the interviews, and others are seriously ill.

The interviews were tape-recorded and varied in length from one to seven hours. No formal questionnaire was used. Questions were open-ended, usually, to avoid a possible source of bias. Before the interviews began, the general topics to be discussed were outlined. Comments and questions, during the course of the interviews, were kept to a minimum and were used often to encourage the flow of ideas. This was done by asking for clarification, where necessary, or by summarizing ideas or feelings expressed by the leaders. These techniques were used largely at the beginning of the interviews and, typically, questions declined in number as the interviews proceeded.

The first four interviews were exploratory and were discarded after the purpose and plan of the study became more clearly defined. These interviews took place with leaders active in other aspects of the socialist movement in this country, and it was decided, finally, to limit the analysis to leaders of the Socialist Party.

Not all interviews were tape-recorded. In two cases there was a mechanical failure in the recording apparatus, and in one case permission to record was not given.

Some time after the interviewing began, the problem arose of guaranteeing anonymity to the respondents. In the initial interviews this was done. After completing several interviews, however, I agreed to contribute the tapes of the interviews to the Oral History Research office, provided I could obtain permission to do so from my respondents. All of the leaders, with one exception, agreed. They were assured that they would not be quoted by name, either by myself or other writers, without written permission.

As far as it was possible to tell, this new factor did not have an inhibiting effect on the content of the interviews. This was true also of the presence of the tape recorder—a small portable unit which was placed in an unobtrusive location. After the first few minutes of conversation, there was rarely any evidence of awareness of the recorder, and to all appearances the leaders became absorbed in their reminiscences.

The settings in which the interviews were conducted (the homes and offices of the leaders) were comfortable, but not luxurious. Furnishings were usually worn and unpretentious. Books predominated everywhere, even in the smallest apartments, rows of books, often from floor to ceiling. Autographed photographs or portraits of past or present leaders of the Party hung on some walls.

Where wives of the male leaders were present at the interviews they listened closely and seemed strongly identified with their husbands' political interests.

In the homes of the very oldest leaders, one had the feeling of being directly in touch with the distant past. The rooms were darkened and still. The interviews reflected, in terms of spontaneous relative emphasis, a preoccupation with the earliest years of political activity—a period of great optimism for these respondents and for the Socialist Party.

As much as was possible, leaders in each of the different generations were interviewed consecutively during a particular period of time, so that whatever similarities these leaders shared would be more apparent. In the months over which the interviews were spread, my thinking about the data tended to be colored by the predominant ambience of the particular set of interviews I was conducting.

The very oldest leaders exhibited a tranquility and equanimity that comes, perhaps, from being outside the arena of daily strivings, surprises, and disappointments. The optimism of this generation set the tone of the interviews with them, and it was infectious. The interviews left me with the ebullient, if momentary, feeling that all will be well in the world, someday. It was not difficult to imagine the almost magical persuasiveness that these leaders must have wielded in their heyday of political activity by the intensity of their beliefs. The deep certainty was still present for many of them and was evidenced, sometimes startlingly, by a sudden and dramatic rise in the volume of their speech and the intensity of their gestures, as they began to speak of the future of socialism, toward the end of the interviews. In their perorations, the memory of long years of failure and frustration often receded in the face of visions of ultimate victory. Man, the undaunted and indomitable, prevailed in life, as he has in literature from Odysseus, to Don Quixote, to Candide.

With each succeeding generation, the pervading tone of the interviews changed. Speech was faster, time was shorter, and amenities such as coffee breaks were increasingly curtailed.

The Interwar leaders did not possess the confident serenity of the oldest leaders, nor were they as busy and hurried as the younger leaders. A feeling of sadness permeated the atmosphere of the interviews with some of these leaders—a mood that was absent in the interviews with the older and younger generations.

It was not until all of the interviews were completed and I had before me the hundreds of pages of typescript that I was able to feel the detachment about the material which was necessary for the exacting and often tedious task of content analysis, involving the codifying, rating, and tabulating of the responses.

Because of my feeling of involvement during the course of the interviews and my desire to have a test of the reliability of my judgments in rating the responses, an outside judge from another discipline was asked to perform an independent, content analysis of the data. Dr. Florence Schumer, a psychologist at New York University, applied the coding scheme I had worked out to the interview materials (the coding variables appear in Appendix B). Dr. Schumer was not informed of my generational hypothesis. Agreement between us on the ratings was high, indicating that the content analysis procedure was a reliable one.

Not all the wealth of material collected was used. As a sociologist, my interest was in the effects of social location, particularly the effects of age and generation, on the thinking and behavior of the leaders. It would be quite possible for an historian, a political scientist, or an economist using the same interview materials to select and organize the data quite differently—and to write quite different books. The multiple worlds of reality are paralleled by the multiple perspectives of the various social sciences.

APPENDIX B

CODING VARIABLES[1]

CODING VARIABLES FOR CONTENT ANALYSIS

1. *Age*

2. *Education (Highest Obtained)*

C–4++	Professional degree, e.g., M.D., Ph.D., Law degree, etc.
C–4+	College graduate, plus some graduate work
C–4	College graduate
C–1+	Some college-level study
12	High-school graduate
< 12	Some high school, but did not graduate
8	Completed eighth grade
< 8	Less than eighth grade

3. *Current Marital Status*

   Married
   Divorced
   Widowed
   Single
   Separated

4. *Country of Origin*

   United States
   Russia
   Other, specify

   [1] The list of coding variables does not necessarily reflect the sequence in which the information was obtained in the actual interviews.

5. *Religious Background or Affiliation*

Jewish
Protestant   Specify denomination
Other   Specify denomination

6. *Occupation (Whether or Not Retired, Major Occupation During Life)*

Official or functionary in non-profit service, political organization, or party, e.g., labor organizer; official in Socialist Party; civil rights leader; union research or educational director; etc.
Professional, e.g., lawyer; minister; teacher; professor; economist; social worker; engineer; etc.
Writer, journalist, editor, etc.
Business
Other, specify

7. *Current Status as a Socialist (Relationship to Socialist Party)*

Is socialist; still member of the Socialist Party
Not a socialist in any sense
No longer member of the Socialist Party, but regards self as socialist ideologically
No longer a socialist, but professes vague, pro-socialist feelings

8. *Primary Influences with Regard to Decision to Join the Party*

NOTE: Any single respondent can be listed in more than one of the following categories, if appropriate.
Economic injustice or deprivation, observed
Economic injustice or deprivation, personal and experienced
Socialization: family influence
Socialization: peer influence
Exposure to leaders
Exposure to ideas, reading
Psychological factors: adolescent rebellion, loneliness, etc.
Neighborhood milieu, community "atmosphere"
Other

9. *Age at Joining Socialist Party*

10. *Occupational Status When Joining Socialist Party*

Manual laborer; factory worker
Student
Other, specify

11. *If Full-time Party Functionary, Age at Becoming So*

12. *Were There Irrational or Psychological Factors in Decision to Join Socialist Party?*

Yes
No
Don't know, no information

13. *Reasons for Failure of Socialist Movement in this Country*

NOTE: Any single respondent can be listed in more than one of the following categories, if appropriate.
Wealth of nation, natural resources, prosperity
Fluidity of class structure; "class struggle" inappropriate thesis
Failure to capture labor movement or working class; ideology inapplicable
Poor leadership of the Socialist Party
The two-party system; electoral system; primary system
New Deal and other capitalistic reforms
Factionalism and splitting within the Socialist Party
Pacifistic stand, or Party was repressed because of stand on war
Ethnic vs. native cleavages; "foreign ideology"
The "American Dream"
It did not fail
Other, specify

14. *Present Conception of Socialism*

Traditional definition, collective ownership
Government control and planning, but not ownership
Extension of the "Welfare State"
Vaguely defined as moral or ethical concept
Other, specify

15. *The Future of Socialism*

Inevitable, not redefined
Inevitable, but redefined as government control and planning
Socialism anachronistic; no longer absolutely necessary; has failed;
    is not inevitable; will not develop
Third party movement may emerge in crisis situation which would
    replace Socialist Party
"We have it; it's here!"
Other, specify

16. *Do you Believe in Realignment?*

Yes
No
No information
Other, specify

17. *If Response to #17 is "Yes": Why?*

Only realistic alternative; only politically effective means
It is a desirable and appropriate means.
Other, specify

18. *Major Social Problem(s) Facing Us Today*

NOTE: Any single respondent can be listed in more than one of
    the following categories, if appropriate.
War
Unemployment
Automation
Poverty
Civil rights
Population surplus
Leisure
Fascism
Urbanization
Materialism
Lack of human values
Other, specify
No information

19. *Attitude Toward Soviet Union; "Stalinism"; or Communist Party in America*

Negative
Neutral
Positive
Other, specify
No information

INDEX